JOINING HANDS

From Personal to Planetary Friendship in the Primary Classroom

RAHIMA CAROL WADE, M.ED.

Illustrated by
MICHELLE ARCHER

ZEPHYR PRESS
Tucson, Arizona

JOINING HANDS
Grades K-4
© 1991 Zephyr Press, Tucson, AZ
ISBN 0-913705-58-6

Illustrations: Michelle Archer
Editor: Susan Newcomer
Book Design and Production: Sheryl Shetler

ZEPHYR PRESS
P.O. Box 13448
Tucson, AZ 85732-3448

Contents

❖ Contents

$\boxed{\text{A}}$cknowledgments

I wish to acknowledge the contributions of many people to the development of *Joining Hands*. The comments and suggestions of the teachers who reviewed the manuscript in its early stages were invaluable. *Thank you* to Lois Wolf, Cathie Hamilton, Henry Maier, Jean Vye, Maggie Symonds, Barb Requa, Betsy Presley, Irene Hillger, Phyllis King, Judy Walp, Anita Gast, Carolyn O'Grady, and Frank Iuro. Special thanks go to Dr. David White at Keene State College for his guidance in an extensive revision of this work.

The Sunbow Community provided loving support for the development of this work and specifically for the quilt project chapter. I am grateful to Lou Halligan for her friendship as well as her permission to use her drawings to illustrate the quilting process.

Thank you also to Patti Driscoll Styles of the Western Massachusetts Consortium for Global Education for ideas used in the *Child's Play* chapter.

My small circle of friends and loved ones have given me inspiration for this work. I could not have completed this book without support from my husband, Jeff, and our children, Mira and Anders.

Bringing this book to its final stage was a joyful, cooperative process thanks to the assistance of my editors, Jane Brewster and Susan Newcomer, and my illustrator, Micha Archer.

Finally, I wish to acknowledge the many children I have taught and with whom I have been friends. Their love and joy in classroom life are what this book is all about. Often, images of the smiling faces of my Milton Elementary School kindergarten children would be with me as I wrote. It is to these children that I dedicate this book.

Introduction: Why Friendship?

Friendship is a word the very sight of which in print makes the heart warm.
—Augustine Birrell

Friendship is a word rich and mysterious. Each of us has a unique understanding of what friendship is, based on a multitude of experiences, some sad and disappointing, others warm and uplifting. Yet, whatever our personal notion of friendship, we are all compelled to seek out and understand the ways it affects our lives. Friendship cannot be avoided. Our successes or failures with it are part of the human experience.

Our true friends bring out the best in us. They guide us toward our highest ideals. They motivate us to develop greater abilities to communicate, cooperate, and love. With our friends we find the courage to seek ways to resolve conflict and to express gratitude. Friendship calls forth our hidden strengths and helps us develop trust and sincerity. To have a true friend is the greatest gift; to be a true friend is the path to reaching one's potential in life.

Having a successful friendship involves a variety of skills. We learn to respect and consider the needs of another person while being honest and true to ourselves. We work at becoming dependable and trustworthy while learning to open up to and trust another. Skills in communicating are vital, as is the willingness to be patient and understanding.

FRIENDSHIP IN THE CLASSROOM

Friendship in the classroom is a powerful dynamic that affects both self-esteem and the ability to learn. A child who feels disliked by the other children will not have the positive, relaxed attitude necessary for optimal learning. When one is upset it is difficult to think clearly. As teachers we need to become aware of the social and emotional dynamics in our classrooms to facilitate both academic learning and children's general well-being.

We need friendship in the classroom to help counteract the fast-paced changes in our culture that have left many children feeling anxious, confused, and lonely. Because of our changing family constellations and because as a culture we move more often than our grandparents did, it is not uncommon for a child's friends, school, and neighborhood to change frequently.

Children define themselves and their values in relation to the people and institutions around them. It is easy to see how some children become confused about who they are and what is important to them. The culmination of this confusion may come in adolescence, an increasingly difficult stage in which growing numbers of teens are feeling overwhelmed and some are even terminating their lives.

FRIENDSHIP IN THE WORLD

When daily life seemed troubling in the past, youths could look to the future for greater peace of mind. As children look ahead for hope or security today, however, the realities of the larger world more likely diminish their dreams, not encourage them. The problems on earth are overwhelming. The scope of hunger, poverty, species destruction, and environmental pollution extend beyond the boundaries of any one nation. We have reached a point in our evolution as a species where interdependence and cooperation are essential for our survival.

If we look at the needs of our world, we find that the lessons of friendship are just as relevant. The crises we are now experiencing on a planetary scale are demanding from us the same abilities that a personal friend does. To solve these problems, larger than any one culture or nation, we must learn to communicate, to cooperate, and to consider others' needs as well as our own.

IMPORTANCE IN EARLY CHILDHOOD

The study and development of friendship has a special role to play in early childhood. The preschool and primary school years provide many children with their first experiences of learning how they can best interact with others outside the family. In these years children first learn what it means to be a friend or how it feels not to have one. At this age children are open to learning the skills needed to communicate, resolve conflicts, and cooperate with others.

The teacher plays a vital role in establishing a peaceful and friendly classroom. The teacher who values friendship with children creates an air of harmony and cooperation that brings joy to daily classroom life. Treating children with respect, kindness, and understanding eliminates many of the reasons why children misbehave and greatly enhances their ability to be active, curious learners.

In accepting the responsibility to teach our children about friendship, we open up a world of possibilities. We play a significant role in contributing to each child's self-esteem and to his or her potential for healthy social and moral development. We do our part in contributing to a healed world, and in the process we grow as well. We cannot honestly teach our children about friendship without first becoming aware of our own attitudes and actions. We must consciously focus on our relationships with children and model the qualities and skills we are trying to teach. This is not a simple challenge, but it is worthy of our time and energy.

The ideas and activities in *Joining Hands* have been designed to help you discover what friendship has to offer you and the children in your class. Included are exercises, games, activities, and projects that encourage children to share the best part of themselves. The Appendix has blackline masters for easy reproduction to accompany these activities and a resource section with suggestions for further reading. The journey begins with a personal exploration of the meaning of friendship and then winds its way through relationships in the classroom, curricular applications, and the extension of friendship into the larger world. I wish you the best as you delve into the mystery of friendship and all it has to offer.

—Rahima C. Wade

SECTION 1

FOR THE TEACHER

QUALITIES OF FRIENDSHIP 1

*Little friends
may prove
great friends.*
—Aesop

When children are young they learn by imitating others. One of the best ways to teach children the skills of friendship is to be a friend to them. In this chapter we will explore the teacher/child friendship, what it might look like and why it is important.

Friendship between a teacher and a child is not the same as friendship between two adults. Teachers do not depend on children for emotional support or share private experiences with them. Nor should teachers become so concerned with children's liking them that they hesitate to maintain discipline or structure in the classroom.

In a healthy friendship between teacher and child, the teacher models and extends the qualities of friendship to the child. Before looking more closely at the teacher/child friendship, take a few moments to explore your personal conception of friendship in the following activity.

A C T I V I T Y

Think about an adult friend with whom you have a special connection. Write down the qualities that are present in this relationship. How do you feel and act toward your friend? What do you value in this relationship?

Here is a list of qualities that my best friend and I developed together. If you feel our words reflect your own idea of friendship, be sure to add them to your list.

respect	love	caring
happiness	joy	trust
faith	integrity	honesty
empathy	communication	sympathy
consideration	gratitude	patience
forgiveness	acceptance	humor
willingness	understanding	nurturance
sharing	compassion	responsibility
sincerity	hope	kindness
courage	dependability	openness

Each of us has an individual conception of friendship. It is important to note that friendship is not a static list of defined qualities but a process or way of being that changes as we change.

How many of these qualities could be present in a teacher/child relationship? Although five- and six-year-olds may not be able to exhibit some of these qualities, they are all accessible to the teacher's interactions with children. Bringing these qualities to classroom life assists rather than detracts from the teacher's role as guide in a structured learning environment.

Friendships are often bonded more closely between people who are similar, who share the same values or interests. No doubt the children in your class are different from you in many ways. Their intellectual development, values, interests, and activities may seem to be totally unlike yours. Perhaps the only things you have in common are your basic humanness and the shared experiences of your daily lives in the classroom.

What a wealth of commonality this is! In one school year you will share approximately 900 hours with a group of people who have the same basic human needs and desires, fears and longings, as you do. Every human being wants to be happy, feel appreciated, and enjoy learning. Almost all of us fear rejection, avoid disappointment, and hope for success and recognition. In addition, you probably share some common interests and activities with your children that you do not recognize. The enjoyment of music, trees, the ocean, airplane rides, and ice cream transcends age differences.

QUALITIES IN THE CLASSROOM

A closer look at the qualities of friendship in a teacher/child relationship shows the unique and varied ways these qualities might be revealed. I have taken some characteristics from my earlier list and given some examples of how they could be lived out in the classroom. As children emulate the adults in their world, much of this behavior and these feelings will become part of the children's daily lives.

Respect

The teacher values children as people and acknowledges their contributions and ideas. When children ask questions or make comments that seem off the subject, the teacher gently redirects their thinking or follows their lead for a while. The teacher deals privately and lovingly with children when sensitive issues or personal problems arise. Gentle reminders are given in the presence of others but children are not scolded or humiliated publicly. Teachers respect children's feelings and privacy when they encourage but never demand a response.

Honesty

The teacher is honest about both the joys and irritations felt with children. The teacher does not deceive children to manage their behavior. If the teacher is feeling tired or upset about problems outside school, these feelings are shared in an appropriate manner. It would be inappropriate to explain all the details of a personal problem, but it is important to say at least "I'm having a hard time today because of something outside school." Teachers also show honesty by apologizing to children when they make mistakes.

Empathy

The teacher attempts to understand what children may be feeling, particularly those who are shy, aggressive, or mean, and to interact with children based on this understanding. The teacher makes a special attempt to *walk in the shoes* of children in the class who have disabilities or who are suffering emotionally and to help the other children understand their special needs. The teacher attempts to learn about the values and lifestyles of minority children in the class and to plan educational experiences that will affirm their racial and ethnic identity.

Patience/Forgiveness

Teachers demonstrate patience and forgiveness with children and themselves, realizing that all of us are learning and working through our own struggles. The lazy, forgetful, or irritating child needs much encouragement and patience to begin to let go of a negative self-image and experience a more positive way of being. The teacher openly expresses forgiveness with the children.

Patience is shown in countless ways as the children often fail to live up to the teacher's standards. However, patience does not become complacency or disinterest.

These are just a few of the many ways that we as teachers can be friends to our students. We are all unique individuals and our acts of friendship will be unique as well.

ACTIVITY

Choose two other qualities from your list of the characteristics of friendship. Describe how you could bring them into your relationships with children.

Friendship lived out through these actions is an ideal to strive toward. In reality we are not the perfect teachers we would like to be, with the right response ready at every moment. As we acknowledge our own and the children's humanity and the difficulties in our lives, we may discover the patience, forgiveness, and courage to move forward. We need to be gentle with ourselves and our children as we try to heal wounded relationships and develop the skills to become better friends.

On a stressful day the whole process of developing the skills of friendship may seem impossible. You may be tempted to give up and take solace in the other strengths such as music, art, or love for books that you bring to the classroom. The time constraints on teaching the required curriculum may seem to preclude any other activities. A difficult child may test your limits. The children may seem to be at odds with your goals when they have endless quarrels with each other or refuse to cooperate.

These challenges mean we must be creative with how we bring the study of friendship to the classroom. I have found many small yet meaningful ways to infuse school life with effective relating. Modeling the qualities of friendship for the children in your class is an important first step in helping children develop the skills necessary for healthy relationships.

2 SHARING IN THE FRIENDLY CLASSROOM

We cannot tell the precise moment when a friendship is formed. As in filling a vessel drop by drop, there is at last a drop which makes it run over; so in a series of kindnesses there is at last one which makes the heart run over.
—James Boswell

How can we bring sharing to our classrooms on a daily basis? To develop friendships with the children as well as among the children, we need to allot time for

- one on one sharing between the teacher and each child
- whole-class and small-group sharing
- conference time for working out solutions to problems in a creative manner

ONE-ON-ONE SHARING

The time we share with children one on one can take place in many small bits and pieces throughout the day.

Before School

There are usually five to ten minutes in the morning when children are coming in, putting their things away, and giving the teacher notes and milk money. This time presents an excellent opportunity for informal sharing. I try to greet the children warmly as they enter the room and talk with a few of them about their family happenings, vacation plans, or dreams as the others put their things away. I do not have a chance to talk with all the children during these few minutes, but it is a good beginning.

Lining Up before and Coming In after Recess

Opportunities for sharing may also occur at other times during the day when the children are getting settled, lining up, or washing their hands for lunch. Any time a few children are waiting is a time you can use to converse with them.

During Academic Learning

Sharing genuinely about a story, a social studies lesson, or a science project can also be a means for developing friendships. For these brief exchanges, you can circulate to different children while the class is working. In my room I find time to mingle and talk with individual children while the class is at learning centers or working on an art project. It is true that for many lessons this type of interaction would be disruptive—during a spelling test, for example. Use your judgment in deciding which activities would be enriched by a little dialogue.

Break Time

I do not advocate giving up all your recess and planning times. However, occasionally you may need to stay in the room to pour paint, staple papers, or engage in some other relatively simple task during which you could talk with a child or two. Young children often enjoy the treat of being invited to stay inside and share with the teacher.

These are the times I use for one-on-one sharing with children. All of these may not appeal to you or you may have other opportunities as well. Explore the variety of ways you can share with children. Besides talking you can play, read, build something, or work on a project together. With a shy child it is often easier to develop a friendship in the process of doing something.

I do not make a point of trying to get to every child each day, or even to have equal friendships with all. Some children may need and pursue the relationship more than others. It is natural for a teacher to have a certain affinity for a few children. Although I am not always successful, I try to have a friendly relationship with every child and to spend a little extra time with the children who I think need it the most.

ACTIVITY

Choose a reading lesson or a social studies topic you will be teaching soon. How can you incorporate one-on-one sharing in this lesson?

———————————

GROUP SHARING

We can plan for the whole class and small groups to share during the school day in many ways. This type of sharing not only will aid in the development of friendships but also will help to establish a harmonious, cooperative atmosphere in the class as a whole.

During Academic Learning

Children can work on math, spelling, reading, or other subjects with a partner or in small groups. Many excellent books on cooperative learning exist. Chapter 5 also describes cooperative learning at the primary level. Research shows that not only do children increase their academic skills when they learn cooperatively but relationships in class also improve.

Story Time

Most teachers of young children read to their classes at least once a day. Try choosing some of the books in Chapter 9, *Learning Friendship through Books.* When the story is over, ask children to share some of their personal experiences with friendship that are similar to those in the book.

Journal Writing

Some teachers have children begin the day by writing in their journals. As you read children's entries later, you can make written comments. You could also ask a few children to share a concern or a joy they have with the whole class. Even young children who have not learned to write can keep picture journals. (You may also want to give children the option of making private entries that you would not read.)

Class Meetings

Class meetings can be held to plan field trips and projects, air concerns, and express appreciation. When children help plan the activities in their class they usually develop a much greater sense of respect and belonging. Dreikurs has developed some excellent guidelines for planning and running class meetings that are listed in *Resources* in the Appendix.

Rule Making

If one of our goals is to give children the experiences and motivation to become active, empowered citizens, then it is important to begin the process of empowerment in the classroom. Creating class rules can be an opportunity for children to develop a sense of responsibility for their behavior and for the standards they must abide by.

Rather than present a complete list of rules and consequences on the first day of school, the teacher should involve the children in the process. It would be difficult to set up rules cooperatively the very first day, however, before you have a chance to build relationships with the children. I had a disastrous experience with this once. The children all knew each other from the previous year and they ganged up against me, requesting some very unreasonable rules.

My suggestion is to create a list of just a few rules and consequences and present this to the class. Explain that in a few weeks the class will have a meeting to decide what is working and what changes need to be made. Children will usually be surprised and pleased that you trust them enough to include their ideas.

What rules are appropriate for the few you present? The best rules are those that clearly relate to keeping order, encouraging learning, and fostering friendship. Two good questions to ask are:

- What rules do we need to interact with each other and our environment with care and respect?
- What rules do we need to facilitate teaching and learning?

You could post these questions somewhere in the room to remind the children that rules serve a positive purpose. Encourage them to think about other rules that may be helpful. Here are some rules you could begin with:

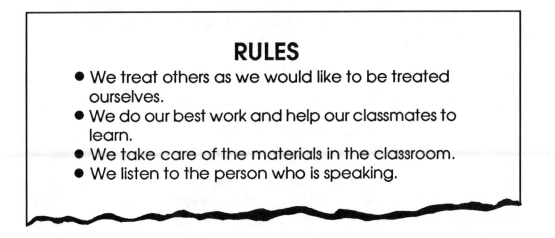

RULES
- We treat others as we would like to be treated ourselves.
- We do our best work and help our classmates to learn.
- We take care of the materials in the classroom.
- We listen to the person who is speaking.

Explain to the children what consequence will result when a rule is broken. (See pp. 28-30 for a description of logical and natural consequences.) When meeting with the children to revise the rules, emphasize that effective rules help us work together cooperatively.

Decision Making

Children have a greater sense of belonging and respect in a class where they are involved in making decisions. One way to foster in children a sense of classroom ownership is to have children design the room. Explain to them the importance of including private work space, a meeting area, and places where they can collaborate with friends.

Children will also enjoy helping to plan seating charts, bulletin board displays, helper lists, topics to study, and rewards. You may have other ideas for ways that your children can become involved in decision making. Even three-year-olds can offer ideas for class parties and field trips. Through shared planning you will be giving children the opportunity to develop skills in decision making, communication, and cooperation.

ACTIVITY

Think about your class rules and the ways you involve children in decision making. Write down at least one idea you plan to try soon.

CONFERENCE TIME

Even in the most well-managed and friendly classroom problems will arise. Children bring many problems with them from home. Although children's misbehavior may arise from feeling mistreated or unimportant in the classroom, there may be other causes. A recent divorce, a new baby, or a missed breakfast can lead to inappropriate behavior, as can more serious psychological or emotional problems. When children test their limits and our patience, conflict results.

We need to have some conference time in our schedules to resolve the conflicts that occur between us and individual students. During school hours we can confer with a child when the rest of the class is engaged in an independent activity. Some possible times for holding conferences are:

- silent reading time
- learning center time
- free play time
- desk cleaning time
- during class chores
- while washing hands for lunch
- during any lesson or assignment for which you have given directions and the class can function on its own (for example, a simple art project, penmanship paper, or seat work)

You may not be able to hold all your conferences during these activities. Occasionally you may need a longer period of time such as a planning break or time after school. As your conference skills and the friendly atmosphere of the class develop, you will probably find that the need for conferences decreases.

Before beginning a conference, take a few moments to reflect on your feelings, on the child, and on the possible reasons for the child's behavior. Consulting with the child's parents and answering the following questions may also be helpful.

- Is this recent behavior that may be caused by stress or is it a pattern that has existed in earlier school years?
- Are classroom activities meeting the child's academic, social, and learning-style needs?
- Is the child disinterested, struggling, or unchallenged?
- What are the child's relationships with others in the classroom?
- What are your feelings in response to this child? Anger? Frustration? Fear? Disappointment?
- If this child had been sent to teach you something, what do you think the lesson might be?
- To what purpose are the child's actions aimed? Can you identify a message or a cry for help this child may be sending you?
- Look back at your list of the qualities of friendship. How many are present in this relationship? How could you include more?

A C T I V I T Y

Take a few moments to think about a child with whom you have had a difficult relationship. Use the previous questions to explore the situation. Note any insights or useful ideas.

_____

Talking alone with a child about a problem may be a new experience for you or the child. Go slowly and remember that discomfort is a natural by-product of dealing with conflict. Hold a conference when you and the child are no longer angry. A calmer moment is always better.

A good way to begin the conference is by sharing why you have asked the child to talk with you. You can express your feelings of irritation or disappointment at the child's behavior while affirming that you believe you can both work together to resolve the situation. Ask to hear the child's feelings. Perhaps something is going on at home or school that is causing the behavior. It is possible that the child may not share with you. Children are often shy or fearful about sharing their feelings with adults, especially if they have been treated disrespectfully before.

Brainstorming Ideas

Before discussing ideas to solve the problem, ask if the child would like to change his or her behavior. If the child genuinely wants to change, you can begin to brainstorm ideas. If the child does not want to change or is unsure, you can discuss the positive aspects of changing. You can explain how he or she might feel better, have a better friendship with you or others in the class, or develop better personal control.

Sometimes it is wise to end the conference at this point and give the child some time to think about what you have discussed. Resume the conference in a day or two. You may find that the problem has lessened or even disappeared even though a solution was not agreed on. If the child feels cared for and feels some power or control over the outcome, the child may decide to change on his or her own. If not, you can work out a solution together at this time or decide what you need to do about the situation and explain it to the child.

Brainstorming ideas to solve the problem is, ideally, a mutual process. Sometimes, however, a child will come up with punitive ideas such as "you can spank me if I do it again" or "you can make me stay in from recess for a month." Show appreciation that the child has shared an idea but explain that you do not want to cause hurt or embarrassment, that you want to come up with some action that will help rather than punish.

Solving the Problem

After a number of ideas have been generated, try to agree on a solution to the problem. Confirm your mutual decision with a handshake, a written contract, or a hug if you like. Be sure to follow through on the agreed-upon plan. Even if the child does not exhibit the undesirable behavior again, check in with the child privately to say how well he or she is doing. Ask if the child would like public praise in front of the class or in the form of a note home.

Some children may resist participating in solving the problem. The teacher is ultimately responsible for keeping order in the class, as well as helping the child. At times you might need to make a decision on your own and let the child know that you plan to implement it, even without agreement. In such instances, it is important to remember that regardless of the child's willingness to participate, your attitude can still be one of friendly guide.

Many techniques can be used to resolve conflict. Some plans motivate the child with rewards. Free time, playing games, or *good day* awards are some of my favorites. Another technique is to use a secret signal, such as a wink or scratching the chin, as a warning or reminder. Children may often improve their behavior when temporarily separated from their peers. I have known children who at times prefer to isolate themselves so they can complete their work on time without distraction.

Another successful technique I have used can be applied to many situations. I ask a child who misbehaves or disrupts the class to help me do something. I say to the child, "Since you made my job harder by . . . , you can help to make it easier by . . . ." The helpful task might be cleaning up the room, sorting through markers or crayons, putting game pieces back where they belong, or cutting out items for a bulletin board.

I have noticed that the reasoning behind this arrangement makes sense to children. They do not feel that they are being punished. It is important that you do not talk to the child while the work is being done. This might be reinforcing. You do not want the child to continue to misbehave in order to stay in and chat with you.

Even though they do not like the inconvenience of giving up some time at recess or after school, children generally feel good about themselves when they have finished helping. Because they end the experience with a positive feeling rather than a residual self-concept of *bad boy* or *bad girl*, they are likely to behave well for the rest of the day.

LOGICAL AND NATURAL CONSEQUENCES

It has been my experience that if I build in a lot of one-on-one and whole-class sharing, the amount of conference time I need will be small, provided that I also have a positive system to manage behavior. (Many excellent books and programs explain such systems, some of which are listed in *Resources* in the Appendix.) In my system, I use lots of appreciation and encouragement with logical and natural consequences for misbehavior.

Logical Consequences

An example of a logical consequence is the child's giving me some of his or her time. A logical consequence is an action that follows reasonably from the misbehavior. Some other examples:

Problem	Logical Consequence
A child is late to class.	The child must make up the work missed during recess, free time, or after school.
A child is bothering others.	The child must sit alone so others will not be disturbed.
A child does not finish a math paper before gym.	The child must finish the paper before going to gym.

Natural Consequences

A natural consequence is an action that flows naturally as a result of the problem with little intervention on your part. Natural consequences are not as easy to use as logical consequences because many situations do not have a natural consequence. A few examples:

Problem	Natural Consequence
A child forgets to bring special project supplies from home.	The child cannot participate in the project.
A child is often mean to others.	No one picks the child for a group project so the child must work alone.

Each situation and each child are unique so it is difficult to define the appropriate consequence for a particular action. Logical and natural consequences teach children that a social order exists in the classroom that will cause them inconvenience if they do not follow it. In this way life becomes the teacher and children build up less resentment against the teacher for enforcing the rules. (Dreikurs's *Logical Consequences: A Handbook of Discipline* (1971) and *Maintaining Sanity in the Classroom* (1971) give more guidelines for using this system in the classroom.)

Regardless of the plan or techniques you use, it helps to have the agreement of the class so that the plan feels like *our* plan. Children often have excellent ideas about classroom management that they have learned from other classes. Also, they are more in touch with how the minds of children work. They will be pleased when you include their ideas.

ACTIVITY

Think about a behavior problem that often occurs in your class such as lost homework or unfinished assignments. What kind of logical or natural consequence could you use in an attempt to resolve this problem?

———————

SECTION II

FOR THE CHILDREN

FRIENDSHIP FOR YOUR CHILDREN

There is a magic in the memory of school-boy friendships; It softens the heart, and even affects the nervous system of those who have no heart.
—Benjamin Disraeli

We must look at friendship through the minds and hearts of young children to discern what qualities and skills we can expect them to learn. Sometimes a need will be clearly evident. A classroom of children who always try to get the best crayons or toys for themselves, for example, could definitely benefit from activities designed to foster sharing.

At other times, it may seem difficult to choose the most appropriate skills or qualities to teach. An important way to create realistic expectations is to understand children's developmental processes. According to psychologists such as Piaget, Kohlberg, Damon, and Selman, children in the preschool years are generally egocentric; in the primary years, they begin to be more aware of others' feelings and ideas. This transition includes a concern for the principles of equality and cooperation.

33

As teachers, we play an important role in guiding young children's transition to this second stage. Social interaction and the principles of friendship will encourage this transition. We need to be sensitive to the fact that we will have children at different stages in our classrooms. Some will be acting with primarily egocentric concerns. Others may show interest in cooperating and playing fair.

We need to be patient with our efforts to foster sharing and cooperation. This behavior will be difficult for some children. We can assist children in the earlier stage by pairing them for activities and projects with children who are more advanced socially.

The findings of these psychologists also have implications for the use of rules and authority in the classroom. Children in the egocentric stage tend to accept adult authority without question. Therefore, we need to be respectful in the way we use our power and thoughtful about what kinds of rules we use. With older children, we can build on their developing interests in equality and cooperation. We can focus on being responsive to their concerns about whether a rule is fair and help them further their ability to hear and understand viewpoints different from their own.

Since young children are just beginning to develop the ability to be true friends, we must start with the most basic skill development. Although the areas that follow overlap in many ways, they also offer distinct and important opportunities for class activities.

- **Communication**
  This area includes speaking and listening skills as well as the qualities of respect and caring.
- **Cooperation**
  This area includes the ability and willingness to share as well as the skills and qualities of communication.
- **Conflict Resolution**
  Resolving conflicts successfully requires the ability to communicate and cooperate. Also essential are the skills of creative thinking and problem solving as well as a belief in the value of peaceful relationships.

The study of friendship cannot exist without these three components. Communication skills are the building blocks for relating to others. Cooperation gives us the means to share activities to create common bonds and feelings of caring and acceptance. Conflict resolution is necessary to work with the inevitable struggles and disagreements that occur in relating with others.

Should we wait until the children have mastered communication before moving on to cooperation? Definitely not. Although these skill areas can be placed in a hierarchy for the purpose of analysis, in practice they reinforce each other. All three are essential in developing the skills of friendship. Chapters 4, 5, and 6 will provide many ideas for how the "3 Cs" can coexist peacefully with the "3 Rs" in our classrooms.

4 COMMUNICATION

When friends ask, there is no tomorrow.
—Proverb

Children come to school with varying abilities to communicate. Some have been exposed to many social situations and have experienced excellent skills on the part of their caretakers. Others may have spent many hours watching television or been with adults who did not model effective communication skills. Young children often learn by imitating the adults and others in their world. We can teach children much about communication by modeling appropriate speaking and listening skills ourselves.

Respect

The first principle in communicating effectively with young children is respect. For the most part, young children are excited about sharing with others. Children who have a good measure of self-esteem will share willingly and openly with the teacher after a "getting-to-know-you" period. The way that we respond to children can either foster or inhibit their desire to share. (Many of the ideas in this chapter are inspired by the work of Dreikurs, Dinkmeyer, and McKay. A number of their excellent works are included in *Resources* in the Appendix.)

What most children want when they communicate is someone to listen, understand, and accept their feelings. If we choose instead to nag, criticize, advise, or lecture, we will not be encouraging our children to share with us. Although we may not always agree with children, we need to respect their thoughts and feelings. When children want to talk at inappropriate times or offer ideas that run counter to the purpose of a discussion, we need to redirect their sharing sensitively and respectfully or offer another time to discuss their important idea.

Nonverbal Communication

Attention to nonverbal behavior is also critical for good communication. Children may send out nonverbal cues in their body posture, facial expression, or tone of voice that can help us understand how they are feeling. A young boy in my kindergarten class gave his parents and me a strong message that he was not ready for all-day schooling when he developed a stomachache every morning.

This is just one example of the many ways children can cry out for help without using words. Most nonverbal messages are more subtle such as hunched shoulders, a sad face, or uncharacteristic withdrawal from sharing. When we notice this kind of behavior we can check in with children to see if they want to talk. Sometimes they will not and we will need to respect their privacy. Children's sensing that we are concerned about their feelings in itself may be enough to lift their spirits.

Our nonverbal communication is important too. We need to be aware of using eye contact and postures that say to children, "I'm listening." Although my knees suffer occasionally from this belief, I think it is important to talk with children at eye level rather than looking down on them.

REFLECTIVE LISTENING

Two specific skills we can develop ourselves and teach children are *reflective listening* and *I messages.* Reflective listening is a technique in which the listener paraphrases, sums up, or feeds back what he or she believes the child is expressing or feeling. It lets the child know someone is listening and understanding. Begin by asking, "What is this child feeling?" Below is a list of words to think about. It is best to try to be specific and to avoid overusing words like *upset* that could refer to many different feelings.

angry	anxious	bored
disappointed	discouraged	embarrassed
frightened	guilty	hopeless
hurt	left out	miserable
rejected	sad	unhappy
unloved	worried	
appreciated	confident	excited
glad	great	happy
loved	pleased	proud

After you think you know how the child is feeling you can offer a tentative response. Here are a few examples of how reflective listening might take place in the classroom.

Child: *I don't want to do this anymore. It's not any fun!*

Teacher: *You sound like you're getting bored with this. Maybe it's time to change activities.*
or
You look discouraged. Is this work difficult?

Child: *Johnny is a creep!*

Teacher: *Did Johnny hurt your feelings?*
or
You look angry. Did you and Johnny have an argument?

It is important to offer your ideas as questions or possible thoughts rather than as foregone conclusions. Reflective listening is a skill that takes practice. Children can begin to learn this skill by playing the following games.

A C T I V I T Y

Reflective Listening Charade

One child acts out a feeling using only facial expressions and body language. The other children try to guess what the first child may be feeling. Encourage the children to share a number of possible answers and point out how many of our words for feelings are similar.

One child makes a simple statement that has strong emotion behind it. Young children can be whispered these phrases by the teacher. Older children can make them up or read them on cards given to them. (See p.169 for a list to use.) The other children try to guess the feeling behind the statement. Allow many possible answers.

These are fun learning games, but children may not practice reflective listening skills in daily classroom life unless you encourage them to do so. Cooperative learning activities and conflict resolution procedures offer many opportunities for children to try to respond to the feelings behind our nonverbal and verbal behaviors.

MESSAGES

The I message is a tool for sharing feelings about another's behavior without placing blame. Three components make up the I message:

1. Describe the behavior: "When you . . ."
2. State your response to the behavior: "I feel . . ."
3. State the consequence of the behavior: "because . . . ."

Here Are Some Examples:

- When you leave your jacket in the hallway, I feel annoyed because someone might trip over it.
- When you leave the paints out, I feel upset because they may dry out and have to be thrown away.
- When you call Joey names, I feel sad because that hurts his feelings.
- When you finish your paper, I feel happy because we can all walk to recess together on time.

It is not important always to use this particular sentence structure. It could become artificial. The lesson of I messages is to remind us to state our feelings without blame and to share with children how the consequences of their behavior affect our feelings. I messages are particularly useful in conflict resolution when it is easy to revert to blaming others. Here is a simple activity for teaching children about I messages.

ACTIVITY

I Message

Write on the board: "When you . . . I feel . . . because . . . ."
Copy and cut apart the cards on p.170 in the Appendix. Give one card to each child and have the child try to construct an I message for the situation represented on the card. Have children share their statements out loud. This activity is probably too difficult for kindergarten children, but second and third graders should be able to do this if you offer some examples first.

You can also assess children's abilities to create I messages by having them complete the worksheet on p.171.

_____

Kindergarten and first grade children can begin to develop the notion of I messages by simply sharing their feelings. Tell children that it is better to say "I feel . . ." than "You . . . ." This will encourage children to express and accept responsibility for their feelings. You can modify the board activity above for young children by writing just the words "I feel . . . ." on the board and using the situation cards on p. 170.

The development of listening and speaking skills is naturally integrated in a classroom where children share and work cooperatively. Many of the activities in *Joining Hands* focus on communicating with others. It is important to note that communication skills are not mastered in a year or two and then left behind for other academic pursuits. Listening and speaking effectively are skills we refine throughout our lives. They are a part of every facet of our world. Early childhood is an important time to begin to develop these building blocks of friendship.

COOPERATION

If we would build on a sure foundation in friendship, we must love our friends for their sakes rather than for our own.

—Charlotte Brontë

Every teacher wants children to cooperate. Without cooperation in the classroom, children and teachers would be constantly at odds and life would be miserable for everyone. All classes encourage children to cooperate with their teachers and the rules in the class. Cooperation is also recommended on the playground, while waiting in line, and in sharing special equipment and materials.

Yet cooperation is often neglected when we come to academics. Children are frequently told to keep their eyes and ears to themselves, not to look at others' work or give them answers, and to work quietly.

An approach to developing both social and academic skills simultaneously is cooperative learning. The research of Johnson and Johnson, Dishon and O'Leary, Cohen, and others unequivocally points to the benefits of cooperative learning in the classroom.   Children not only profit academically from this kind of learning, but they enhance their social skills as well. Children who have spent significant amounts of time working in cooperative groups develop more tolerance and understanding of others. Friendships begin to transcend the boundaries of racial, ethnic, and gender differences.

COOPERATIVE LEARNING IN A SECOND GRADE CLASS

The principles and techniques of instituting cooperative learning with young children are shown through the following experiences of mine with a second grade classroom.   Most of the eighteen second graders in this class had been together since kindergarten so they knew each other well.   They were generally cooperative with each other, but they were accustomed to working individually during academic activities.   Their classroom teacher and I developed this project together.   It was the first time either of us had tried cooperative learning.   We decided to focus their first cooperative learning experiences around learning to tell time.

 **Day 1**

We begin by having children work with just one other child.   This is challenging enough and ensures participation of both children in the activities.   I put up on the wall a large poster of rules for working with partners.   (The poster is shown on p.172 in the Appendix.)   We discuss the two sayings on the bottom of the poster: "We sink or swim together" and "Two heads are better than one."

I tell the children that they will not be working with their best friend in the class, that their teacher and I have decided who will be partners. (Creating heterogeneous pairs—boy/girl, high/low abilities, different races—has been shown to benefit all children academically and socially. Even the high ability students learn as much or more than if they were working individually.) Before we tell the children their partner's name, we discuss the importance of not hurting others' feelings by saying "awww" or frowning. The children do a good job of accepting their partners.

Each pair is then given one pencil and one paper to complete. (This is called *positive resource interdependence*. Children need to cooperate; they are not able to simply do their own worksheet separately.) This first paper, found on p. 173, was designed not to teach telling time but to teach the concepts of sharing and support. I wanted to give the children a simple exercise they could complete successfully, which they did. The students have fun discussing and underlining the answers. The better reader in the pair helps with difficult words. During the children's work the teacher and I circulate and observe. I am generally pleased with their first experience in cooperative learning.

When they are finished, we discuss the papers and give them feedback about the different ways we saw cooperation taking place (taking turns underlining, discussing, sharing the reading, and so forth). Although most of the children did very well, I note in my journal that Ron and George had a hard time beginning to work. Ron is a new child in the classroom, and George is the most popular boy.

Some of the children are confused about how to help their partners. Many spout what they have heard for at least a year or two: "You can't give the other person the answers." We talk about ways to help without simply telling the answer to your partner.

 **Day 2**

The teacher gives one small clock to each pair of children. After an introductory lesson, they spend time guessing times on the hour and on the half hour. John, a bright, gregarious little boy, yells at his partner Susie, "Well, come on, don't take forever. Just guess!" Overall the children still do not know how to help each other without giving each other the answers.

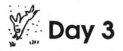 # Day 3

I give the children a copy of the *25 Ways* worksheet on p. 174. We talk about the importance of working together, just as you might on a baseball team. It is spring and most of the children love sports, so they enjoy the analogy. We discuss how you can't take someone else's turn at bat, but you can encourage them, praise them when they get a hit, show them how to hold the bat, and console them when they strike out.

The children then play a game with the worksheet. As they work on their clock times, they try to say as many different statements as possible. They seem to enjoy supporting each other. I take John and George aside and talk with them about how they can better work with their quieter and slower partners by using lots of encouragement and praise (plus a healthy dose of patience!).

 # Days 4 - 8

The teacher sets goals and bonuses for the children. These goals are set individually, according to the children's abilities. The goal is what they can attain if they work reasonably well. The bonus is what they can achieve if they give their very best effort. Many of the children's goals are to tell time to the half hour or quarter hour. The bonus might be to tell time to the minute. For a slower child, the goal might be to tell time to the hour or half hour and the bonus to the quarter hour.

One day they have a longer time to work in pairs and one pair comes up to the teacher and says, "Are we going to stop soon? We're getting sick of this." On another day there is no time for practicing with partners and the children are disappointed. Occasionally the teacher has a hard time getting the children to listen after cooperative learning time.

 **Day 9**

Today the children work with flash cards. They are all doing well. I hear lots of supportive comments as I circulate among them. George is being much more assertive and keeping Ron at work. The teacher and I both feel that we gained a lot more work time from the children today by having them practice in pairs. They are also learning their times.

 **Days 10 - 13**

The children continue to learn and work well. One day they play a game as a class and score points with their partners after they work on a pencil and paper exercise by themselves. Ron scores a lot of points, and George is thrilled!

 **Day 14**

The teacher calls me at home to report that the children *all* met their goals and *all* got their bonuses! The teacher believes that the children learned more through this approach than they have in other years. (Although the children have practiced and worked together many times, they take a written test individually so the teacher can assess each child's learning.)

 **Day 15**

All the children are happy and excited about sharing their success with me. We present new partners for the next project. Some of the children are enthusiastic about changing, and some say "awww." John wants to stay with Susie! "I was just learning how to work with her," he says.

These experiences point out some of the principles as well as some of the pitfalls in initiating cooperative learning in the classroom. Many more ideas and procedures for using cooperative learning exist. In-service training on this method is usually helpful as are the books in *Resources* on p. 203. The ways to structure cooperative learning are various. Although such learning is similar to traditional group work, significant differences must be carefully planned for.

The teacher has a key role to play not only in planning cooperative learning experiences for the children but also in surpervising their work. While the children are working, it is important that the teacher observe their interactions, encourage them to rely on their partners for support and help, and make notes about what skills they may need to be taught. The teacher should intervene only as needed to redirect a group through the use of thoughtful questions, to give feedback, or to encourage new ideas.

This type of supportive supervision is different from the traditional lecturing, instructing, and disciplining that teachers often do. Partners need to be encouraged to seek out ideas and assistance in their group first before asking the teacher for help.

You will be much more successful with cooperative learning if you teach your children basic communication, cooperation, and conflict resolution techniques first. Although one can focus on many skills and qualities with young children, I focus on the concepts of support and sharing. I messages and reflective listening are also valuable skills for cooperating.

It is also important to spend some time with the children as a group after the activity is completed to discuss their cooperative behavior. Children need to become aware of actions that are helpful and those that are not.

POSITIVE INTERDEPENDENCE

Positive interdependence is the essential component of cooperative learning that distinguishes it from group work. Three main types of positive interdependence are positive goal interdependence, positive resource interdependence, and positive reward interdependence.

Positive Goal Interdependence

Positive goal interdependence takes place when the pair is asked to submit one worksheet or when you randomly choose one worksheet from the pair to grade or one child to take a test for the pair. These measures help to ensure that children will take responsibility not only for their own learning but also for their partner's learning.

Positive Resource Interdependence

Positive resource interdependence occurs when you purposefully limit the pair's materials so that they must cooperate. Examples are giving the pair one pencil, paper, and scissors or giving each child different yet necessary information for the task at hand.

Positive Reward Interdependence

In positive reward interdependence, the pair might receive a group grade or nonacademic reward if both partners achieve certain criteria. With our unit on telling time, because all the children met their goals, we all had a popcorn party. It is essential to include at least one type of positive interdependence in your work with this method.

With young children it is important to begin slowly and teach them the skills to cooperate with success. Sharing is difficult for many young children and one does not want to overtax their attention for working in this way. As their skills and abilities to cooperate successfully develop, they will want to work more in pairs and they will benefit both academically and socially.

6 CONFLICT RESOLUTION

Two persons cannot long be friends if they cannot forgive each other's little failings.

—Jean de La Bruyere

Children are always being told to share, be kind to others, and cooperate. In many ways, however, society reflects the value of competition over cooperation. Our classrooms are often a mirror for society. In many competitive classrooms, children have learned that only a few students will be praised, only one row will win the treat, or only one paper will be read aloud. Even in a cooperatively run classroom, children may be fearful that they will somehow lose by helping their classmates be successful. Their unwillingness to cooperate can be one source of conflict.

However, to have conflicts with other people is also a natural part of relating to others. Human beings have many needs, desires, and goals. When a person's needs or desires are unmet, frustration results. If this lack of fulfillment seems to be caused by another person, conflict ensues. Children need to be taught that conflict is a normal and acceptable part of life. Also, although we may have little control over when conflict occurs, we have many opportunities to affect the course of a conflict through our choices and actions.

Conflicts in School

Conflicts in school can arise for many reasons. Children may need more attention or may be bored with the school program. Some children have a particularly difficult time with sharing or with not having enough space to move in and out of social interactions. Both children and teachers may come to school feeling grumpy. Any time desires are strong and are not being fulfilled, conflict may occur.

Often young children will ask the teacher to settle their arguments, prevent a fight, or help make amends for some wrongdoing. One of the greatest arts we as teachers can develop is to learn when and how our presence can best help children in their struggles. The ultimate goal is to have children learn how to resolve their own conflicts with patience and kindness.

We need to be clear and consistent with children about their conflicts. When is it appropriate for them to come to us? Is tattling okay? Do we have a plan for helping children solve their problems? As teachers we must work out these answers for ourselves.

In a class I had a few years ago I allowed children to come tell me about their own problems or those of their friends. They did not seem to engage in excessive tattling, and I wanted them to know that I cared about their behavior in other classes and on the playground as well as in my presence. Some children shared about the shortcomings of others as a way to build up control in themselves. These children resisted getting involved in any conflict and wanted me to know that they were *good.* By telling me about others, they sought approval for not participating and gaining strength to resist again. Other children were so conscientious about following rules that it bothered them to see others not doing so.

Of course, some children tattle for the pure enjoyment of getting someone else in trouble. I would spend some time talking privately with a child who did this and try to give the child more positive attention as this is probably a large part of the purpose of tattling. You need to look at the particular group of children you are working with to decide how you will deal with this issue. Tattling may help you become aware of problems that exist, but it can also create a lot of mistrust and resentment between children.

Whether you allow children to come to you frequently or only for serious problems, the next question is what to say or do. You may suggest that the children work the conflict out by themselves. This is a good idea, provided they can do so effectively. Conflict resolution involves a complex set of skills, yet we can use many tools to help children develop their abilities.

The following activities will guide young children in developing an awareness of conflict and choice. Recognizing the feelings associated with conflict and knowing that a person has a variety of ways to act are important aspects of learning to resolve conflict creatively.

A C T I V I T Y

Conflict Awareness

Discuss with the children conflicts they have at home and at school. Emphasize that conflict can be an argument, physical fight, or uncomfortable feelings that result when you do not get what you want.

Encourage children to express their feelings about conflicts they have had recently. They can paint, draw, role play, sculpt, or dance their experiences.

❀

Help children develop their awareness of conflict by discussing what happens to them physically when conflict begins. Some responses might be "my face turns red," "I get hot and sweaty," "my stomach hurts," or "I can't think right." Have children use the illustration on p.175 to draw how they feel when conflict happens.

———————

Taking the time to focus on an awareness of conflict and how it feels is an important step in the conflict resolution process. Recognizing the onset of conflict gives the child an opportunity to act thoughtfully rather than react impulsively in a difficult situation. Children who do not have this awareness may find themselves becoming so angry that they feel out of control. When children understand the feelings associated with conflict, they can begin to look at the choices available to them.

A C T I V I T Y

All Kinds of Choices

🍎

Read children a story (see the books listed under Books on Friendship in *Resources* on p.210) or perform a short puppet show illustrating a familiar conflict. Stop the story or play in the middle of the problem and have the children brainstorm about what the characters involved could do. Save their ideas on a large piece of paper or on the blackboard. (Exercise no judgment at this point about which choices are appropriate. At this stage children simply need to develop the awareness that they have the power to choose.)

Discuss the idea of choice. Emphasize that we all make choices many times during the day, including during times of conflict. Help children become aware that they choose to act a certain way in school and at home. They may argue strongly that you or their parents make them act in particular ways, but show them that actually they almost always choose their actions while considering the probable consequences. Discuss the possible consequences for each choice you have listed and the feelings that might result from each action.

Have each child draw or paint a picture showing a choice he or she might make in response to the conflict shared earlier. Have them write or dictate to you a sentence that describes the picture. Make a book of these pages to use when situations of conflict arise.

Here is one way to use the book. Tommy has just come in from recess and is angry with Jennifer. After the children have calmed down, have them sit together with the book of choices and find a picture of an action they could have taken or could take now in response to their conflict.

After the children have worked with the idea of choice to the extent that they recognize they have the power to choose and that many options are available, you can begin to focus on actions that are peaceful and cooperative.

A C T I V I T Y

Positive Choices

Again, use a familiar conflict either on its own or from a story or puppet show. After the children have brainstormed a list of actions they could choose to do, have them pick out the ones that will have a positive, peaceful outcome. Assert that you are now interested in choices that will result in cooperative relating, friendship, and happiness for all the people involved. Deep breathing, counting to ten, and other relaxation techniques that help us let go of anger are positive choices that children may not know unless you teach them. (See the list on p. 62 for other techniques to release anger.)

Have the children make new illustrations using only peaceful ideas for a new book entitled *Positive Alternatives to Conflict.* Use this book to help with conflict resolution in the classroom. Discuss with the children how they feel emotionally and physically when they choose positive alternatives.

Rather than focusing on fights and arguments that occur, give children a special sharing time when they can talk about positive choices they have made in conflict situations and how they felt. This time might be scheduled right after recess or during free time or another time of day when children usually have conflicts.

GLOBAL CONFLICT

When children have learned about conflict and the choices they make in response to conflict in their own lives, they can begin to understand conflict in a broader sense. Although it might seem inappropriate to talk about war or global conflict with young children, they are often aware of these issues through their contact with television and older children.

ACTIVITY

Global Conflict

Use the following questions as springboards for discussion, role playing, and art projects. Ask these questions when you notice children engaging in war play or when children express curiosity about war.

- What is war? What have you learned or been told about it?
- When two people fight, is it like a war? How?
- Why do you think countries in our world fight with each other? What are they afraid of?

Encourage children to brainstorm and draw pictures of a world where everyone's needs are met. Discuss the following questions.

- What things do people need to have a healthy and happy world?
- Why do you think everyone does not get what he or she needs?

Ask children the following questions to help them realize that leaders of countries also make choices.

- What kinds of choices do the leaders of countries make when they have conflicts?
- How do these choices affect our human family?
- Can you think of some *positive choices* in response to conflict they could make?

Emphasize to young children that we all can and do make a difference in the world.

- How could people in the world make more peace rather than war?
- How can we make our world a more peaceful place to live?

Young children may have simple answers to these questions. Encourage the children to learn more and correct their misconceptions. Be careful about giving children complex or troubling information. Accept children's ideas and points of view as valid whenever possible.

Even young children can understand that countries in our world have disputes over land, food, and natural resources and that many people fight and even kill each other in these conflicts. The following activity is a way to illustrate to children that a limited number of resources are on our earth that we all need to share.

Bring in a pie and discuss how to divide it among the class. The children will notice that if a few people get very big pieces, others will get small pieces or none at all. You can use this situation to illustrate the importance of sharing food, land, and natural resources.

STEP-BY-STEP CONFLICT RESOLUTION

All these activities will prepare children to begin to solve conflicts effectively by themselves. Some children may benefit from a specific method or structure to successfully resolve their conflicts; others may not. The following system of picture symbols was developed with young children in mind. (See figures to copy on p.176.) The principles can also be used with older children and even adults.

The symbols are color coded so that one person is red and one is blue. Children each pick a color and then follow the steps by looking at the pictures. I put the symbols on a poster in a corner of the room with a small rug big enough for two children to sit on.

1

The first step is called *centering time.* The two children close their eyes, take a few deep breaths, and become quiet for a moment, centering on how they feel.

2

Red speaks and Blue listens. The red person can say anything about how he or she is feeling or about the conflict itself. The blue person is *only* to listen.

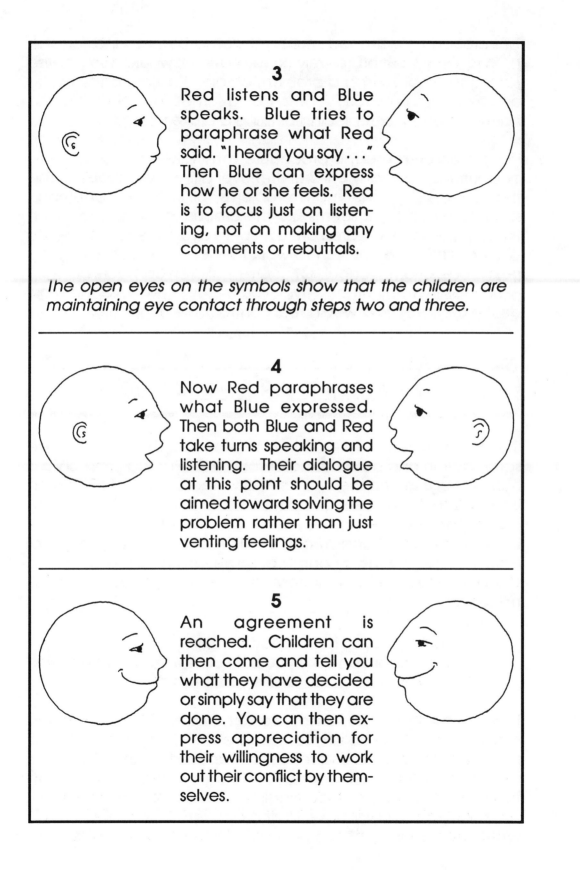

3

Red listens and Blue speaks. Blue tries to paraphrase what Red said. "I heard you say . . ." Then Blue can express how he or she feels. Red is to focus just on listening, not on making any comments or rebuttals.

The open eyes on the symbols show that the children are maintaining eye contact through steps two and three.

4

Now Red paraphrases what Blue expressed. Then both Blue and Red take turns speaking and listening. Their dialogue at this point should be aimed toward solving the problem rather than just venting feelings.

5

An agreement is reached. Children can then come and tell you what they have decided or simply say that they are done. You can then express appreciation for their willingness to work out their conflict by themselves.

This procedure will need much modeling beforehand for children to carry it out effectively on their own. It would also be wise to discuss what *solving a problem* entails. Possible answers are expressing genuine forgiveness, doing something special for the harmed person, or replacing or fixing a broken item.

Having children use this procedure may take time away from academics, but many children fret over a fight with a best friend through spelling tests, math problems, or into their afternoon studies anyway. If it seems like the process is taking too much time, however, or children are using it to avoid their school work, you could require children to work their conflicts out during the next recess or after school. Of course, children can work out their difficulties in many other ways. You might even have the class devise a system they would feel comfortable using.

Teacher as Mediator

Sometimes when children come to me I feel the need to take some action and be a mediator for them. Perhaps one child is hurt and crying and the other is angry. The first thing I always do is attend to the hurt child and make sure that comfort, hugs, or bandages are given as needed. Sometimes the mishap has been an accident and all can be dismissed quickly. If physical harm has been done on purpose, however, I take the child who did it aside and we talk privately. In general, I try to convey three messages:

- It is not okay to harm another person.
- I care about and like you but I do not like your behavior.
- Other ways exist to handle your problems.

I usually ask the child, "What are some other things you could have done besides hurting someone else?" I also try to set up a natural or logical consequence of the child's action, such as "Since you used the jump rope to hit Sam, you will not be able to take the jump rope outside again this week." or "Because you are punching, you will have to sit by yourself for a while. I don't want anyone else getting punched." When the consequence is logically related to the misbehavior and is explained in a loving way, the child will usually understand and not feel resentful. If the hurting is a recurring problem, however, I set up a conference where we can discuss ideas for solving the problem together.

I do not demand that the child who did the hurting say "I'm sorry" to the other child. I feel that when I force children to apologize, I am making them speak insincerely. It is a beautiful experience to watch children apologize in their own time and way. One way that children learn to apologize sincerely is by being in the presence of other children and adults who do so.

If arguments and fighting are common among many of your children, it may be helpful to explore the subject of conflict with the whole class at a calm moment. Here are some questions you might want to discuss.

- What situations are frustrating to you in school?
- When have you had conflict with someone?
- Have you ever been in a fight? How did you feel?
- How did you resolve the problem?
- Does anyone *win* a fight? How?
- When was the last time you were angry at school?
- How did it feel?
- What did you do? What else could you have done?
- What ways can you think of to lessen conflict in our class?

To have an effective, honest discussion, be sure to accept whatever the children offer. Their ideas and values might not be the same as yours, but you will all learn a lot about each other if you are tolerant of differing viewpoints. You may need to remind the children that you are not looking for any right answers and that they will not be graded on their responses. Children enjoy and appreciate the opportunity to express their feelings in an accepting atmosphere.

RELEASING UNWANTED FEELINGS

An important aspect of conflict resolution is the release of angry, sad, or hurtful feelings. Many times this release takes place while solving the problem, but sometimes it is necessary to have the child engage in an activity that specifically focuses on letting go. This is particularly useful in the case of a strong emotion such as anger. Stored up anger and sadness can create physical and psychological problems as well as increase the probability of another angry episode. Some of the following ways to release unwanted feelings will inevitably result in laughter, which is, in itself, a great release.

- Running, jumping, push-ups, sit-ups, trampolining
- Doing an anger dance set to music
- Making exaggerated angry faces
- Verbalizing ("Grr! Aarrgh! I'm angry!")
- Talking to a puppet
- Crying
- Ripping up a piece of scrap paper
- Doing an anger drawing
- Writing "I am angry!!!" in big letters on scrap paper
- Playing with clay
- Punching a pillow
- Relaxing through deep breathing
- Closing your eyes and visualizing a calm, peaceful scene
- Stretching exercises

It is ideal to have a small area where a child can go and be alone for a while to think and release hurtful feelings. A large box with carpet inside is a great place for a child who wants to be alone or who is not feeling well. At other times the box can be used as a playhouse or a space to read in.

Emphasize to children that their feelings are natural and acceptable and that a variety of means exist for releasing uncomfortable feelings if they want to. Do not try to force angry children to relax or assign one of the above activities as a punishment for being angry. Respect the rights of children to feel and act however they choose. Each child is unique. Some of the releasing suggestions may even increase some children's aggression. Observe children's behavior after they have engaged in one of the above activities and make notes for future reference. If you offer suitable releasing suggestions with love and caring, children may take you up on one of the ideas and your friendship will be enhanced in the process.

CREATIVE PROBLEM SOLVING

Another way to help children deal with their problems is to teach them creative problem solving. Creativity is a skill that can be developed through practice and is a useful tool. The following steps show how the creative process can be used to find more effective solutions to problems. The picture cues are provided to help younger children. The examples following the steps will make the process more meaningful.

KNOW YOUR PROBLEM
What is the problem? Gather information about the situation, then state the problem in a positive way. It is helpful to begin with the words, "In what ways might I . . ."

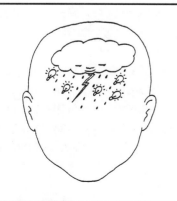

BRAINSTORM
What can I do about the problem? Think of as many ideas as possible. Defer judgment. Include any ideas that come up, even the seemingly ridiculous or impossible.

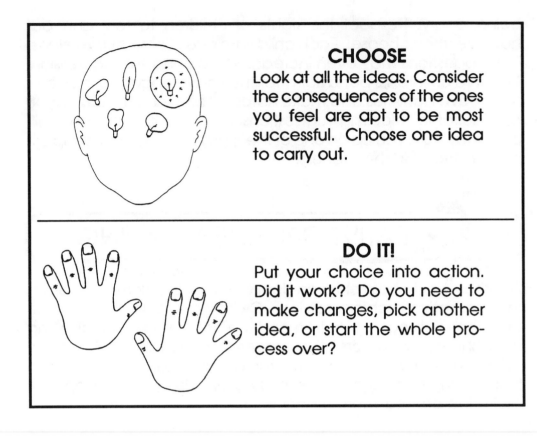

CHOOSE
Look at all the ideas. Consider the consequences of the ones you feel are apt to be most successful. Choose one idea to carry out.

DO IT!
Put your choice into action. Did it work? Do you need to make changes, pick another idea, or start the whole process over?

You will need to guide children through these steps a number of times before you can expect them to use the procedure on their own. Some ideas for presenting these steps for the first time follow.

Step 1 - Know Your Problem

1. Ask children, "How many of you would like to have a life without any problems?" Explain that problems are a natural part of life, that we can never be totally without them, and that you are going to teach the children a system to make it easier for them to solve many of their problems.

2. Ask children to mention a variety of problems they have. Jot these down on the blackboard or a piece of paper for later use. Tell the children that the system you are going to teach them has four steps and will make problem solving fun. Show the pictures of the four steps and read the accompanying text. (You can copy the large symbols on pp.177-180 for this.) Line the cards up on the blackboard or somewhere the children can see them and you can refer to them.

3. Pick one of the problems the children mentioned earlier. It will be easier if you pick a problem that is shared by a number of children. Hold up the first card. Begin by gathering information about the problem. To illustrate the process, I'll use the sample problem "No one will play with me on the playground."

4. Questions you might ask to gather more information are:

- Does it happen every recess?
- How do you feel about it?
- Do you do or say anything that makes others not want to play with you?
- What do you do when no one plays with you?

Coming up with a statement of the problem may seem easy, but it is perhaps the most difficult part of the process. Depending on the information children give you, any of the following could be an accurate restatement of the problem as a question. In what ways might I:

- have fun at recess?
- make new friends at recess?
- get people to play with me?
- feel happy at recess?

5. Try to guide the children in discerning the actual problem rather than choosing a problem statement for them. Sometimes the problem is clear and this step can happen quickly. At other times a little more attention at this stage can help to clarify the problem and enhance the likelihood of finding a successful solution.

Step 2 - Brainstorm

1. Discuss the concept of brainstorming with the children. Our brains create a *storm* of ideas. Emphasize that any idea will be accepted. Children love this step. They cannot give a wrong answer, and it is a lot of fun. If your class is new to brainstorming, you might want to do the following exercise before working with the recess problem.

2. Hold up a simple object such as a pencil, spoon, or cup. Ask the children, "How many different uses can you think of for this object?" At first the children will probably give conventional answers, but as a few children begin to take risks and offer unusual uses, other innovative ideas will surface. Encourage children to build on each other's ideas and be sure to persevere through a quiet period in the process, usually found when the conventional ideas run out and before the more unusual ideas begin.

3. Reasons exist to defer judgment at this step. First, the mind flows creatively with many ideas if we do not stifle it with fear, condemnation, or other restrictions. Second, often a good idea will come to someone in relation to a silly idea. For example, perhaps one child suggests for the recess problem, "Take a rocket ship to the moon." Although this is impossible, it might spark another child to suggest, "Take a ride on a swing" or "Pretend you are in a rocket ship while playing on the monkey bars." This juxtaposition is called *hitchhiking*. Encourage children to share ideas in this way.

4. I usually jot ideas on the blackboard so the children can see that I am including each idea and for easy reference in the next step. Try to use the children's own words as much as possible. For young children, it is helpful to draw a picture of the idea along with the words on the board.

5. Occasionally a few children will use the brainstorming session as an opportunity to become silly or rude. If you have a child or a group that you feel might have this tendency, you might want to discuss the exercise and your expectations for their behavior beforehand.

Step 3 - Choose

1. Before starting this step, discuss the concept of consequence. Children who act impulsively usually completely skip this step in their thinking. If you use logical and natural consequences in your classroom as part of a positive behavior management system, point out some of these examples. Ask the children to consider what might happen if they:

- ran out of the classroom
- lost their lunch money on the way to school
- gave someone in their family a present
- watched television all day for a week
- stayed up very late on a school night

When the concept of consequence is understood, return to focus on the recess problem.

2. Have the children choose four or five of their favorite ideas for the recess problem, then discuss the consequences of each. There are no right answers, only probabilities and possibilities.

3. In addition to discussing each consequence, you can rate the ideas according to certain criteria. I often use a grid. An example for this problem is shown below.

	Easy	Fun	Safe
Play with a ball	yes	no	yes
Get someone to play jump rope with me	no	yes	yes
Go on a swing	yes	yes	yes

This helps the children recognize which ideas have the most likelihood of success. Ask the children to pick one solution they would like to try.

Step 4 - Do It!

1. It helps to set up a specific time to carry out the proposed solution, and the sooner the better. In this case, the next recess would be perfect.

2. Afterward, discuss whether the solution worked. You can always return to any of the previous steps and try again.

3. Post the symbol cards in an area where they will be visible to you and the children. Make sure to go through the process again as a group sometime soon and probably at least twice more in the next few weeks. These demonstrations can be briefer because the children are now familiar with the steps. Encourage the children to use the steps on their own and share their results with the class. Support them in their efforts.

4. You can also teach the children this simple song to the tune of "Row, Row, Row Your Boat" to aid them in remembering the steps:

> Know your problem, brainstorm,
> Choose, and do it, too.
> If you take these simple steps,
> You'll see your problem through.

FRIENDSHIP IN THE CURRICULUM

A friend is a present you give yourself.
—Robert Louis Stevenson

Many opportunities exist for incorporating the study of friendship into the curriculum. In social studies, children are taught about families, neighbors, community helpers, and historical events. The qualities of friendship play an important role in each of these areas. Many of the stories teachers read to young children also deal with the trials and triumphs of friendship. You can even focus on friendship with spelling, penmanship, and language arts. In addition to integrating friendship studies with these subjects, you may also want to teach a specific unit on friendship.

The following units will give children an understanding of friendship through language arts, social studies, science, music, and art.

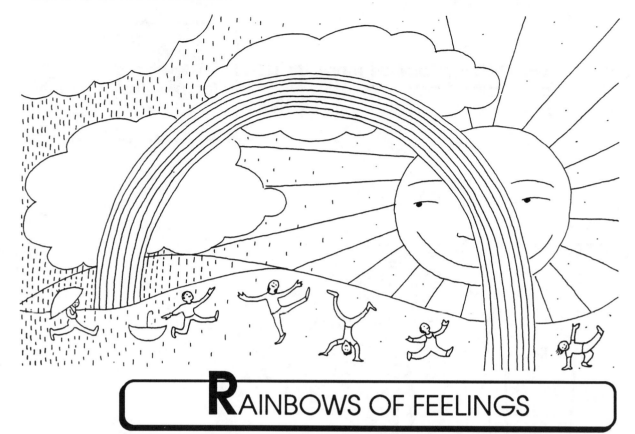

RAINBOWS OF FEELINGS

A rainbow is a wondrous phenomenon from our natural world that can help teach children about their emotions and getting along with others. Life is not always *sunny*, but we can learn to shed some light on our *rainy* moments and emerge into new growth and awareness.

Sometimes our *rainbows* can be brought to life only by confronting and dealing with our limitations and conflicts in a loving way. We can teach children that inner frustration with ourselves and difficulties with our friends are not problems that should not exist but rather opportunities to learn about self-acceptance and communicating with others.

The rainbow unit might be used at the beginning of the school year when children are concerned about making friends or adjusting to a new teacher. You may also find that this unit fits in with lessons you teach—on spring or the weather, for example. I often combined the rainbow unit with teaching the colors in kindergarten.

An attractive bulletin board display is a good way to introduce the subject. I collected pictures of different rainbows, many from old calendars.

The following activities provide many ideas for learning about friendship through rainbows. The first two activities focus on the scientific aspects of rainbows. The next four activities explore connections between rainbows, feelings, and conflict resolution. The last four activities involve the arts.

Rainbows of Feelings

Skills: communication, critical and creative thinking, conflict resolution
Qualities: insight, sharing, kindness
Subjects: science, language arts, music, dance

Discuss rainbows. Look at the different pictures on the bulletin board. What is different about each rainbow (size, location, double or single rainbows, brightness)? What is similar (the color spectrum, colors in the same order, the curved shape)?

Add a sign to the bulletin board that says:

SUN + RAIN = RAINBOW

Discuss how rainbows come to life. Sunlight is made up of all colors. A mist of water can bend the rays of light so that the colors become visible. The seven colors in a rainbow are red, orange, yellow, green, blue, indigo, and violet, but most people see only four or five of the colors. You can experiment with creating your own *rainbows* using prisms, crystals, puddles, or sprinklers plus sunshine. You may also see the rainbow colors in glass door knobs, cut glass objects, or soap bubbles.

Talk about *sunny* feelings and *rainy* feelings. How are they different? Encourage children to share their personal experiences. Play a game of charades in which a child pantomimes an experience. Let the class guess whether it was a sunny or a rainy moment.

Explore with children the notion that by adding some *sun* to our rainy moments we can create something new and beautiful in ourselves and our friendships, just as the sun and the rain create a rainbow. Role play some of the ways we can be kind to someone who is hurt or unhappy. Have a *Make a Rainbow Day*. During the school day children can keep a lookout for some *rain* they can add their *sun* to. At the end of the day, children who tell about the *rainbow* they made can receive a rainbow sticker or badge (use master copies on p. 181).

Talk about the times when children have difficulty with each other. *Thunder* (yelling and angry words) and *lightning* (hitting, pinching, or other striking blow) can result from our *stormy* encounters. How can we bring some *sun* into these difficult times? Have children brainstorm ideas for how they can bring *sun* to their conflicts. Children can then draw or paint their favorite ideas.

Overcoming problems in ourselves or resolving disagreements with friends gives a special joy and sense of victory that could not be experienced without having the difficulty in the first place. Discuss with children the special joys that have occurred in their lives by the presence of certain problems. Make puppets and create special *rainbow plays* of these experiences to share with others.

Have children create their own rainbow pictures to add to the display on the bulletin board. (You can use the outline on p.182 for this purpose.) Children can draw their favorite environment or activity beneath the rainbow or draw a scene that shows friendship. Also discuss and then draw the weather conditions that would probably be present when the rainbow appears.

Have children use watercolors. Using the colors of the rainbow, let them draw arcs of red, orange, yellow, and so forth, painting them *on top of* each other. All the colors will blend together, making a muddy color. Then have children paint arcs *next to* each other, as in a rainbow. With some explanation and discussion, children will have a visual picture of why it is wonderful to be different (races, gender, values) and how we all complement each other.

Find pieces of music that reflect the mood of the sun, the rain, and a rainbow. You might even involve the children in classifying different pieces. Make a tape of a few minutes each of rain, sun, and rainbow music and have students create dances to illustrate *The Coming of the Rainbow.*

If your class becomes enthusiastic with this area of study, they could form a Rainbow Club with the purpose of creating rainbows by bringing some *sun* to *rainy* situations in your class, school, or community. The experience of planning and persevering to triumph over a difficult situation will give them more strength and insight to continue to create rainbows in their own lives. *Resources* on p. 205 lists books on rainbows for children and teachers.

PLANTING LOVE

When warmer weather appears and summer is just around the corner, children want to be outside more and may find it difficult to continue to adapt to the normal school schedule. I always try to take my children outdoors more at this time of year for learning activities and field trips. Also, I find this planting love unit helps them to direct their spring energy toward becoming closer friends and creating a harmonious atmosphere in our room.

Many science units for spring focus on planting seeds and watching them grow. Following are some ideas to combine with these experiments to enrich children's understanding of the qualities of friendship.

ACTIVITIES

Planting Love

Skills:	cooperation, creative thinking
Qualities:	interdependence, sharing, patience
Subjects:	science, art, language arts, music

In the process of planting seeds and growing plants, children can explore the following qualities of friendship. As the children see how the qualities manifest themselves in the plant world, they can compare their knowledge with how these qualities exist in our friendships. These questions may be useful to stimulate discussion, art projects, or role playing.

Interdependence
Plants - What do plants depend on in their environment? Why do animals, insects, and other beings depend on plants?

People - Whom do you depend on from day to day? Whom do you depend on once a week or a few times a year? Who depends on you? Why does this person depend on you?

Sharing
Plants - Think about the things you mentioned that are interdependent. What does the earth share with the plant? What happens when the sun shares its rays? What would bugs do without leaves or flowers do without bees?

People - What do the people in your life share with you? What do you share with them? What would your life be like without them? What do you think your friends' or family's life would be like without you?

Cooperation

Plants - The sun, earth, water, and you all work together to help the plant grow. They cooperate because no one of them could care for the plant without the others. What do you think would happen if you tried to grow a plant without water or light?

People - Discuss or draw a picture of an activity in your life that involves the cooperation of a few people. Could you do it all by yourself? Why or why not? Would you want to try?

Patience

Plants - Do you ever wish your plant would hurry up and grow? Plants grow in their own time, in their own way. We can help the plant by providing the best conditions for its growth—sunlight, clean water, mineral-rich soil, and fresh air. And patience!

People - Discuss the frustrations you feel in your effort to become a better friend or your difficulties with how others treat you. What *conditions* can you create to help your growth? Can you develop more patience? What might help you to do this?

Create a tune, hand movements, or a dance to these words:

> Kind hearts are the gardens,
> Kind words are the roots,
> Kind deeds are the blossoms,
> Kind love is the fruit.

Discuss with children how we help love to *grow* by developing kind hearts, words, and deeds.

This activity will help students become aware of their friendly words and actions. Give each child a copy of p.183. Have them write their names on the lines inside the flowers and then cut apart the six sections on the dotted lines. Each time they say or do something kind for another person during the day, they give that person one of their flowers. The object is to give away all six of the flowers by the end of the day. Before going home, sit in a circle and discuss the kind words and deeds that were exchanged.

This activity focuses on a bulletin board display of an apple tree (see p.184). Cut out a large tree with many branches but no leaves, apples, or roots. Have the children cut out and write their names on the roots and blossoms found on p.185. Coloring them will add to the attractiveness of the display. At the end of the day, children who shared a kind deed can pin one of their roots beneath the tree. Blossoms can be put up by children who remember kind words they said. This activity can go on for a few weeks until one day a surprise occurs. Some apples appear on the tree with children's names who have been very kind. The class will enjoy watching a few *love fruits* appear each morning.

For a list of children's books on plants, see p. 206 in *Resources.*

ALPHABET QUALITIES

In the primary grades, teachers usually spend a fair amount of time working with the alphabet, teaching letter names and sounds, penmanship, spelling, and library skills. You can easily include friendship in this area by incorporating the study of friendly qualities along with other letter activities. A list of positive qualities follows—some for each letter of the alphabet—along with several suggested activities.

A - awesome, amazing, aspiring, affirming, accepting
B - beautiful, brave
C - calm, compassionate, caring, creative, courageous
D - determined, delightful, diligent
E - empathetic, enthusiastic, energetic
F - funny, fearless, forgiving, friendly, faithful
G - graceful, genuine, generous, grateful
H - hopeful, honest, heroic, helpful, happy
I - innovative, intuitive, instinctive, interested
J - jovial, just, joyful
K - kind
L - loving
M - merry, majestic
N - noble, neat, nice
O - optimistic
P - polite, persevering, peaceful, patient
Q - questioning
R - respectful, reasonable
S - sincere, sympathetic
T - truthful, triumphant
U - understanding
V - victorious
W - witty, willing, warm, wonderful, wondering
X - excited, excellent
Y - yearning
Z - zestful, zippy

This list can be used in a variety of ways. You may want to study a quality as you are learning that letter's name, sound, or formation. Another possibility is using these words along with whole language or writing activities. Older children could use the quality as a spelling word or as the basis for a paragraph or story. You could study one quality a week or one a day or use them all in a unit on alphabetizing. A simple plan for using these qualities follows.

ACTIVITIES

Alphabet

Skills: communication, creative thinking
Qualities: numerous: whichever ones you choose
Subjects: language arts, art

Pick one quality for each letter—the term most familiar to your children or the term most unfamiliar to increase their vocabulary. The children could also pick the one they want to work with, or perhaps the class as a whole needs to develop certain qualities that could be discussed.

To develop the children's understanding of friendly qualities, have them take turns describing themselves or each other in a positive way. You may find that they have a tendency to use physical characteristics such as pretty, tall, or brown haired rather than personal and emotional characteristics. Encourage the latter and contribute plenty of examples. Susan is joyful, Frank is generous, and so forth. This exercise could be done at the end of your study of friendly qualities, perhaps using only the qualities you studied.

Each week or day that you work with a new letter, introduce the quality by writing it on the board and discussing what it means. Children will enjoy sharing their stories of being brave or understanding, and listening to each other's experiences will make the quality more alive and meaningful than any dictionary definition could.

Encourage the development of the day's quality by noticing children who demonstrate it. I spent a week once observing which qualities I noticed in children. I was surprised to find out that 90 percent of my observations concerned being *quiet* or *good listeners*. Encouraging a variety of qualities is important for the development of friendly children.

Make individual or class booklets in which children illustrate all the qualities listed. At the top of each page, write a sentence for each letter such as "A is for appreciation." Children can dictate or write short stories describing their pictures. Lines on these pages could also be used for penmanship practice.

Have everyone spend a day looking for people who demonstrate a particular quality. At the end of the day, children can discuss the acts of forgiveness, optimism, or other such quality they observed.

With each new quality, find a way to have the class share in an experience that will make the quality alive for them. Here are some possibilities, one for each letter of the alphabet.

> **Accepting-** Have everyone share his or her favorite food, sport, or storybook. Encourage the children to accept each other's opinions even when these opinions are different from their own.

> **Brave-** Have each child say why he or she likes another child.

> **Creative-** Have children write a story or draw a picture about the future.

> **Determined-** Children can try to make string figures (see p.186). If they make mistakes, have them help each other and keep trying.

81

Empathetic- Have children sit in pairs. One child tells about a sad or difficult experience while the other child listens carefully.

Forgiving- Say to the class, "Is there someone at home or at school with whom you feel angry? Try to forgive that person today."

Generous- Say, "Share something that you have brought with you today with someone else in the class." Children could share a toy, a favorite pencil, a hat, a library book, a hug, or a smile.

Helpful- Say, "See if you can find some way to be helpful today without being asked. Look for something you can do in the classroom for someone in need."

Interested - Say, "During our science lesson today, show that you are interested by asking a question."

Joyful- Play a game in the classroom that everyone will enjoy.

Kind- Say, "Say some kind words to an adult in the school today."

Loving- Say, "Give one of your friends a hug today."

Merry- Have an un-birthday party!

Nice- Say, "See if you can be nice to everyone in our class today."

Optimistic- Say, "Tell us about an upcoming event you are looking forward to."

Patient- Have the children make a list of all the times during the school day they can practice patience—while lining up, for example, waiting for lunch, or sharing toys. Have them practice!

Questioning- Say,"Ask someone in our class whom you don't know very well something about himself or herself."

Respectful- Discuss the golden rule: *Do unto others as you would have them do unto you.*

Sincere- Say,"Tell someone whose feelings you may have hurt that you are sorry."

Truthful- Have the children draw pictures about a time they were scared.

Understanding- With partners, have the children talk about a time they were upset. Have them try to understand why their partners were so unhappy.

Victorious- Have the children learn to master a challenging skill such as balancing books on their heads or repeating a short poem.

Warm- Say,"Smile at as many people as you can today."

EXcited- Have the children pantomime how they act when they are very excited.

Yearning- Say,"Is there something you have been wishing that you had for a long time? What is it?"

Zestful- Say,"See how many times you can hop on one foot while holding a friend's hand."

A display of different alphabet books is a nice complement to these activities. See p. 206 for some of my favorites. At the end of your studies, discuss with the children which qualities are most important in friendship.

FRIENDLY HELPERS

Many social studies curricula in the primary grades include a unit on neighborhood or city helpers. The following activities focus on the importance of friendship in helping roles.

ACTIVITIES

Friendly Helpers

Skills: communication, cooperation, conflict resolution, critical and creative thinking

Qualities: interdependence, helpfulness

Subjects: social studies, language arts

❀

Collect hats that are worn by various professionals (police, firefighters, construction workers, nurses, and so forth). Have children wear the hats in the following role play. One child picks a hat and plays the role of a neighborhood helper. This child must come up with a problem to act out that can be solved by another helper. Children can try to guess which helper's skills are needed and then one child can play that role to complete the skit. Some examples that could be used are:

- A construction worker gets hurt on the job and needs a nurse or a doctor.
- A dentist's office is robbed and the police are needed.
- A nurse buys an old house that needs some work and calls a construction worker.
- A teacher's car breaks down on the way to school and a mechanic is called for help.

You can make this activity more challenging by copying and cutting apart the cards on p. 187 and having a pair of children draw two cards. They would then create the problem-solving skit with their two characters.

As a follow-up to the previous activity, children might enjoy drawing cartoons or writing stories based on their favorite skits.

Have students list all the qualities they feel are important in certain occupations. For instance, a nurse needs to be gentle and a firefighter needs to be courageous.

Discuss why it is important for neighborhood helpers to be friendly toward others. Does it affect their ability on the job? Is it good for business? Which helpers would have an especially difficult time doing their job if they were not friendly?

The handout on p. 188 will reinforce the concept of interdependence. Have the children write the name or draw a picture of a community helper in each circle. Connect with arrows those workers who might work together or need each other on specific occasions. For example, imagine there has been a car accident. A man is hurt. The police need a mechanic to tow the car and a doctor to help the hurt man. The doctor needs the nurse to help in the operating room, and so forth.

8 FRIENDLY HOLIDAYS

True happiness consists not in the multitude of friends, but in their worth and choice.
—Ben Jonson

Celebrating holidays can also provide opportunities to teach children about friendship. Many of the world's holidays have love and goodwill as their essence, but somehow these qualities are often buried under more commercial ways of celebrating. We need to introduce other elements of celebration beyond eating rich foods and receiving gifts for our children to appreciate the true nature of many holidays.

Some children are not permitted to celebrate certain holidays, usually for religious reasons. Check with the children or their parents about the activities you plan to do. Parents may have a favorable response to them, but if not, prepare a neutral activity of a similar nature for that child. For example, if most of the class is designing Halloween costumes, a child could design a costume for a play.

Find out what holidays the children in your classroom celebrate at home. Including activities in your curriculum that focus on holidays celebrated by different ethnic and cultural groups will enrich the education of all your children and increase the self-esteem of the students who celebrate them at home.

The activities on the following pages focus on developing specific skills and qualities of friendship related to holiday celebrations. The last activity for each holiday is designed to reach out to a larger community, our friends throughout the world.

HALLOWEEN

Of all the holidays commonly celebrated, Halloween seems to be the one most associated with greed and unfriendly behavior. Visions of children rushing about to fill their sacks and stomachs full of candy come to mind, as well as fears of harmful tricks.

Halloween was not always celebrated in this manner. In the Middle Ages, it was designated All Hallow's Eve by Pope Gregory to honor all saints who had died. The tradition of Halloween costumes began when poor parishioners dressed up as saints. The following ideas for celebrating Halloween come closer to the original spirit of the holiday.

A C T I V I T I E S

Halloween

Skills: cooperation, creativity
Qualities: respect, admiration
Subjects: art, language arts, social studies

Discuss with children the origin of Halloween and how it compares with the customs we observe today. What is a saint? What qualities did saints manifest in their lives? (Although a *saint* is a religious figure, you can extend the concept to include many people who live good, helpful lives.) Do you know anyone who has *saintly* qualities?

Instead of wearing plastic costumes of their favorite television characters, have children dress up as people from history or from the present who have admirable qualities. The list on the following page will give you some ideas. You may have others to add. You could also include people from your local community. Be sure to tell children that even the most wonderful people have their shortcomings, and in fact, a famous person who is admired by many is often criticized by others.

Florence Nightingale
Mother Teresa of Calcutta
Jackie Robinson
Thomas Edison
Ben Franklin
Robin Hood
Johnny Appleseed
Susan B. Anthony

Abraham Lincoln
Martin Luther King, Jr.
Helen Keller
Luther Burbank
Marie Curie
Paul Bunyan
Lewis and Clark
Chief Joseph of the
     Nez Percé Indians

Young children might also want to dress up as some-one they would like to be, a favorite plant or animal, or a hero or heroine from a favorite storybook.

Encourage cooperation by asking children to bring in clothes, pieces of fabric, or hats for students to use in creating their characters. Be sure to have face paints or makeup on hand for painting faces.

Role playing and dramatic skits can also be com-bined with Halloween costumes. Have children work in pairs to come up with a skit that includes a simple problem and a helpful response that brings about a solution.

Collecting money for the United Nations Children's Fund (UNICEF) is an activity that happens in many countries around the world on Halloween. If you initiate this project, be sure you explain to children where the money is going and why it is so desperately needed. You can obtain free literature and UNICEF cans by writing to the following address:

> U.S. Committee for UNICEF
> 331 E. 38th St.
> New York, NY 10016

THANKSGIVING

Many cultures have traditionally set aside a time to celebrate the annual harvest. Thanksgiving is the most familiar to us and is celebrated widely in the United States.

The first Thanksgiving is generally associated with the Pilgrims, although this is subject to some debate. After a long, hard winter, the Native Americans helped the Pilgrims plant their fields. When the time for the fall harvest arrived, the Pilgrims had built homes, were in generally better health, and had a good crop of corn. The Native Americans were invited to celebrate with them. Food was provided by both parties, and days were spent in feasting, game playing, and contests of marksmanship.

For children to gain a true picture of early American history, the peaceful cooperation between these two groups must be contrasted with later injustices toward Native Americans, such as their being forced many times to leave their homes and move west. You can make this idea real for young children by asking them how they would feel if they chose to share a special toy with another child and then that child took it and kept it.

Many elementary classrooms focus on Indian activities in the fall. It is important not to simplify or stereotype Native American cultures or to present them as a thing of the past. Instead, explore with children the present-day diversity of Native American lifestyles and values. Many of the customs and practices of Native American cultures can teach us valuable ways to relate to and honor the earth and its inhabitants.

You can also celebrate the true spirit of the first Thanksgiving with the following activities focused on gratitude and generosity.

Thanksgiving

Skills: communication, creativity
Qualities: gratitude, generosity
Subjects: language arts, art

Discuss the concept of gratitude. What other words do we use that have the same meaning—appreciation, thankfulness, gratefulness? Ask "What do you feel thankful for?" Another way to ask this question is, "What would you have difficulty living without?"

Brainstorm with children many creative ways to express gratitude. Give each child a homework assignment to express thankfulness to someone. The next day have the children discuss the different ways they thanked someone.

This experiment can also teach children about gratitude. Have children pick something they feel thankful for and then ask them to try to go without it for a whole day. Have them discuss their experiences the next day.

91

Another fun activity for the class is this. Tape the following on an audio cassette and play it to the class:

> You have all been chosen to be spies for the Appreciation Association. Your mission is to keep an ear and eye open to be aware of any thank you or other gesture of gratitude expressed.

Each child should carry paper and pencil to tally the occurrences. See if you can arrange to have children sit in on other classes, the library, the nurse's room, and so forth. It may be helpful to have the children brainstorm a specific list or use the handout on p.189.

Discuss the concept of generosity. Ask if children are being generous if their parent or teacher makes them share something or if they hope to get something in return. Ask what experiences they have had in which they or someone else was generous. Establish that generosity means freely giving to another person of their time, skills, or things.

So often giving is associated with money and objects. Have children list or draw ways they can give of themselves—skills, time, services. Gifts can be given to friends or family by drawing or writing the chosen activity on the gift coupon on p.190.

The helping hands on p.191 can be signed, cut out, and given to others in the class or at home. When someone requests the child's help, a helping hand is returned to complete the exchange.

If children enjoyed tallying observations for the Appreciation Association, they might want to continue the activity by scouting out acts of generosity.

Announce to the children that they are to pretend they have just received one million dollars to spend in ways that will benefit the community or the world. Younger children can draw what they would use the money for; older children can make a list and estimate the cost of each item. Be sure to allow children to discuss what they would spend the money on and why they made that choice.

CHRISTMAS AND CHANNUKAH

Christmas, Channukah, and other festivals of light are celebrated all over the world during the winter months. Almost all these rites focus in part on giving and receiving gifts. Unfortunately, this aspect of celebrating has taken over. Many children are more concerned with the presents that they will receive than with the true meaning of the holidays. The following are some alternative ideas to help young children experience the true spirit of giving.

ACTIVITIES

Festivals of Light

Skills: creativity
Qualities: caring, sharing
Subjects: art, language arts, science

Have a toy exchange. Encourage children to wrap up one of their toys to give to a classmate. In this way they will truly be giving something from themselves, rather than just spending their parents' money. You could also take the toys to a needy family in your community or to a social service agency that coordinates holiday gift giving.

Encourage children to use their creativity in making something from nothing. A card, poem, story, drawing, or painting can provide an opportunity to express caring in a genuine way.

Many useful gifts can be made from recycled or inexpensive materials. Loved ones will appreciate the thought and time that go into such creations.

Nature walks in different locations at various times of year can present a wide range of gift-making materials. Throughout the year, collect nuts, pinecones, flowers, driftwood, seashells, and other objects that you encounter. Bring them out in the fall to begin your creations.

One gift I have successfully made with young children also reflects the holidays' emphasis on light. We first collected baby food jars and cleaned off the labels and glue. We then filled the jars with layers of beans and seeds and other natural objects. After we glued a lid on the top and a second lid upside down on the first, we glued on a votive candle. I recommend using a strong glue such as epoxy or hot melt glue for both lids and candles. This gift makes an attractive centerpiece.

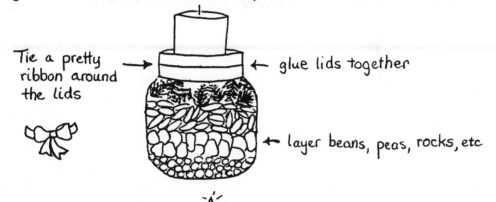

Tie a pretty ribbon around the lids → ← glue lids together

← layer beans, peas, rocks, etc

You can make gifts for hungry birds by smearing pine cones with peanut butter and rolling them in bird seed. Hang the pine cones with string in a favorite tree for your bird friends to enjoy.

Here's an idea to share with parents. If children want to buy presents for others, have them earn the money through small odd jobs around the house or in the community.

To give to your community, your class could organize a schoolwide food bank or clothing drive to collect items for community members. A bake sale or other fund-raising project can raise money for a worthy project or organization. Children are so full of light and love that a visit to a hospital or home for the elderly is a wonderful gift to the people who live there. If your class cannot visit, you could create pictures or cards to send there. Explore other ways with your children to give to the community or the world at this time of year.

———————

These are just a few ideas for enriching your children's experience with gift giving. What is important is not the particular gift, but the involvement the child has in giving it. By sharing time, skills, and creativity, the children give of themselves in their gifts and can begin to realize the joy and fulfillment of sharing.

新年快樂 新年快樂

CHINESE NEW YEAR

Many different holidays are celebrated around the world. The Chinese New Year is similar in purpose to our New Year. It is a time of renewal and good luck wishes. Celebrating a holiday from another culture will help children become aware that almost everyone loves to celebrate and that many wonderful festivals occur around the world.

The Chinese New Year takes place on January 1 now that the People's Republic goes by the same calendar as the West. The holiday used to be observed between mid-January and the end of February, on the first day of the first month of the old lunar calendar. You can celebrate Chinese New Year at either of these times. Following are some traditional customs of the Chinese New Year and some ideas for activities in the primary classroom.

ACTIVITIES

Chinese New Year

Skills: cooperation, communication, creativity
Qualities: blessing, sharing, celebrating
Subjects: art, language arts, math, physical education

Preparations for the holiday begin a week before the actual date by cleaning homes, shops, and factories. Once the New Year festivities start, no cleaning is allowed because some people feel that much luck arrives with the New Year and cleaning might sweep or wash some of it away. A few people even put away knives and scissors for fear that they will cut their good fortune in two. In the classroom, this is an excellent opportunity for cleaning out desks, organizing bookshelves, washing blackboards and windows, and other cleaning tasks we do only periodically. You may even want to store scissors out of sight.

On New Year's Eve, many homes are decorated with red paper signs saying Happy New Year or Good Education. In class, make signs in English or Chinese (see p.192 for the Chinese characters) to put up in your room. Children could take signs home or put some up in other classrooms or around the school to extend the blessings further.

The last meal of the old year is called the Join Together or Reunion Dinner. Traditionally, the extended family sits at a large round table because the circle is symbolic of perfection. Each of the foods eaten at the meal also has symbolic meaning. Something white is eaten to ensure good health, something red to enhance prosperity, and fish to foster good luck in the coming year. Each person must leave a small piece of each type of food on his or her plate. This will ensure that good health, wealth, and good luck will be with one in the coming year. For class, invite children's families to school for lunch or celebrate with your school family— other classes, the principal, art and music specialists, and so forth. Have children come up with a small list of whom they would like to invite. (See sample invitation on p.193.) The list might include older brothers and sisters in the school. A simple way of planning this meal would be to have each person bring his or her own lunch plus a small piece of fruit or a nut that could be left uneaten to bring good luck in the coming year.

A traditional game played during the Join Together Dinner is Rock, Scissors, Paper, which was invented in the Far East and is now played all over the world. Your children may already know this game. If not, here are the directions. Rock, Scissors, Paper is a hand game played between two people in rounds. Each round is won or tied according to which hand signals the children extend. They begin with their hands behind their backs. One child says "one, two, three, shoot" at which time both children bring one hand out to show a hand signal to the other child. The hand signals are shown below.

Rock   Scissors   Paper

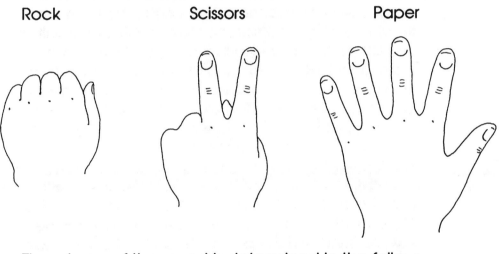

The winner of the round is determined in the following way: scissors cut paper, paper covers rocks, rocks break scissors. For example, if paper and scissors were the two hand signals extended, scissors would win because scissors cut paper. The winner of rock and scissors would be rock, and the winner of paper and rock would be paper. If both children choose the same signal, they tie. Children can develop counting and adding skills by playing a number of rounds and keeping score. For younger children, each round could be worth one point. Older children might have each round worth more points.

On New Year's morning, Chinese children awaken early and greet their parents by saying "Gong ho xin xi," which means "respectful greetings, new happiness." Their parents give them a red and gold envelope with lucky money that they can save or spend as they wish. If they visit other relatives during the day they usually receive more money. For class, give out envelopes to the children and some play money coins (or real pennies if you wish). This activity can be adapted to focus on friendship by having the children go around the room to each other saying "respectful greetings, new happiness." Each time they greet someone, they are given a coin to put in their envelopes. At the end of the greeting time, have the children practice their adding skills by counting the money in their envelopes or put all the money into one large pile and count it together as a class. If you are using real money, perhaps the class could decide a fun way to spend it.

The Chinese do not have to work or attend school during the first three days of the new year. Some preferred activities for these days are going to the movies or the opera, attending martial arts demonstrations and folk dances, walking on stilts, and sharing riddles. For class, plan one special event for the children such as a movie or a martial arts demonstration. See if the physical education teacher can teach the children some folk dances or how to walk on stilts. Get a book of riddles to share.

Many other customs, foods, and activities are associated with the Chinese New Year that you can adapt for classroom use. Although children will enjoy the unique aspects of the Chinese celebration, reinforce the concept that the Chinese and American New Year celebrations are similar in many ways. Both cultures see the new year as a time for renewal and good luck. In both cultures, much festivity, food, and special activities surround the holiday. Playing the game Rock, Scissors, Paper will demonstrate that some of our games and ideas for celebrating are shared in our interdependent world.

VALENTINE'S DAY

Some say the real St. Valentine was a Christian priest or bishop martyred in Rome about A.D. 270 for performing illegal marriages. The story goes that he was held in jail and became friends with the jailer's daughter. On the night before his execution, he sent a note thanking her for her kindness and signed it "your Valentine." That was the beginning of the tradition of Valentine's Day cards.

In most classrooms children exchange small valentines from commercial packets with the rest of the class. Following are a few ideas to make this exchange more meaningful.

ACTIVITIES

Valentine's Day

Skills: cooperation, communication, creativity
Qualities: appreciation, caring
Subjects: language arts, art, writing

If you have a small class in which to exchange valentines, children might be able to make their cards. Provide plenty of scrap materials—fabric, lace, ribbon, and so forth—to encourage original creations.

With a larger class, have children pick the name of one classmate out of a hat and design a special valentine for that person. The card could include pictures of activities that the maker enjoys doing with the recipient. Instead of signing his or her name, the child could provide clues to his or her identity in the form of pictures or words.

A simpler version of this activity is to have each child make one valentine and put them all in a hat. Then each child picks one out and guesses who made it. You might want to display the cards on a bulletin board after they are opened.

Provide time for children to make valentines for special people who have shown them some kindness. Class discussion may reveal a list of people from parents and friends to doctors, community helpers, and neighbors.

♡

Have the whole class get involved in making a card for each child. Place a folded sheet of paper in an envelope for each child and write his or her name on the envelope. Circulate the cards and have the children write or draw something they appreciate about that person on the card. (Remind children to skip the envelope with their own names so they will be surprised when they open the finished cards.) When all the cards are complete, seal the envelopes and put them in a special box until the grand opening on Valentine's Day.

♡

Large, mural-like valentines can be given from the whole class to special people in the school such as the principal, secretary, or school nurse.

♡

In small groups, have children design *A Valentine for the World* illustrating their love and goodwill for the planet. Concern for different cultures, peace between nations, endangered species, or clean air and water could be expressed. Display the valentine posters in your school hallway or in a public building such as the town post office or library.

———————————

MAY DAY

The spring festival May Day, marking the revival of life in early spring after winter, is celebrated in many countries. In medieval times May Day was the favorite holiday of many English villagers. They gathered flowers to decorate homes and churches, sang spring carols, and gave gifts. A special king and queen of May were chosen and everyone enjoyed dancing around the Maypole.

Other countries celebrate the day in different but equally festive ways. In Switzerland and Germany, people plant trees, sometimes outside the home of a loved one. The day is celebrated in Italy by courting one's sweetheart. In the United States, May baskets are hung on the doorknobs of friends and neighbors on the morning of May 1. Following are some ways to have fun on May Day.

ACTIVITIES

May Day

Skills: creativity
Qualities: kindness, celebration
Subjects: language arts, art

Children can gather fresh flowers or make tissue paper flowers and arrange them in paper baskets. These can be hung on the doorknobs of the other classrooms, given to a special friend, or taken to a senior center.

Children could dress up as May kings and queens. Make paper crowns and use old curtains or table-cloths for robes.

Have children create skits that show the kindness and benevolence of a great king or queen.

Invite another class to come and see the skits and join you for May Day dancing and singing.

Write to a school in another part of the country or the world. Wish the students a happy May Day and include tissue paper flowers made by the children. You might want the children to glue their school picture on one of the flower petals.

Talk with the local Chamber of Commerce or mayor's office about where the children could plant trees in the community. Businesses may donate money to pay for this special project if you promise them publicity in the local newspaper and school bulletin.

If you or some of your children celebrate other holidays during the school year, try to research their true beginnings. You will find that most special days originated from an act of love and kindness or from the joy of living and sharing.

LEARNING FRIENDSHIP THROUGH BOOKS 9

A book is a friend; a good book is a good friend. It will talk to you when you want it to talk, and it will keep still when you want it to keep still—and there are not many friends who know enough to do that.

—Lyman Abbott

Many wonderful children's books explore the concept of friendship with all its joys and difficulties. Some books highlight the fulfillment that comes from sharing activities and forming bonds. Some books address the difficult aspects of friendship and how these difficulties can be resolved. Many children's books explore friendship in a light-hearted way with frogs, hippos, rabbits, and teddy bears.

In addition to reading these books to children, you can use book-based activities in a language arts lesson or a creative dramatics lesson. You can also use a book focusing on friendship with a subject you may be studying in science or social studies such as animals or community helpers. You may even be able to use some friendship books to develop a math lesson in counting or addition.

THE GIVING TREE

A controversial book about the give and take in friendship is *The Giving Tree* by Shel Silverstein. The thoughtful story and clever illustrations depict the changing relationship of a boy and a tree. Although the boy grows up and loses some of his love for the tree, the tree continues to give him what she can. One learns of the deep satisfaction and also the sorrow in loving so completely.

Some people feel that this is a tender story portraying the love of a tree for a boy. Others feel that their relationship is too one-sided to be called a friendship, that the tree is simply used by the boy for his own needs. Some have also commented that the book is sexist since the tree, who does all the giving, is depicted as female.

Because the book provokes different viewpoints, it is an excellent one to help explore individual ideas about giving, receiving, and friendship. I combined some of the following activities with a unit we were studying on trees. These activities can be used in conjunction with *The Giving Tree.*

A C T I V I T I E S

The Giving Tree

Skills:	communication, creative and critical thinking
Qualities:	sharing, caring, generosity
Subjects:	math, language arts, art

❀

Read *The Giving Tree* to the class and discuss the story from two points of view—the tree's and the boy's. Ask questions about the tree's point of view:

- How does the tree feel in each part of the story?
- Does her love for the boy ever make her sad?
- Is there anything she is unwilling to give?
- Does giving make her happy?

Ask questions about the boy's point of view:

- How does the boy feel about the tree in each part of the story?
- When does he say "thank you" or show appreciation for the tree?
- Does he give anything to the tree?

Allow children to have their own opinions in response to these questions. Many questions do not have one correct answer. Listen to each child carefully. Their responses will reflect their feelings about giving and receiving.

Have children relate their own experiences to those of the tree and the boy. Here are some sample questions:

- Has your love for someone ever made you sad?
- Can you remember a time when you gave a lot of yourself—time, energy, skills—to someone?
- What is the greatest gift you have ever given someone?
- When did giving something to someone make you really happy?
- Have you ever loved something for a while and forgotten about it later?
- What is the greatest gift someone has given you?

You may need to talk about the concept of gift as more than a tangible object. Love, smiles, hugs, and sharing are all gifts we give each other. *Greatest gift* might be defined not only as something that gives the recipient a lot of happiness, but also as something with which the giver is involved. You can use the tree as an example. She gives gifts of herself rather than items she has purchased.

Have children pantomime parts of *The Giving Tree* while you read. Afterward, discuss how they felt in their roles.

On another day, have children think about what they would do differently if they were the characters in the story. Act out some of the new scenes.

Discuss the idea of change during a friendship. Children could share or act out their experiences of having a friend change. Here are some questions to guide the discussion:

- Have you ever had a friend who is not your friend now?
- What happened? Why aren't you friends anymore?

As children offer their ideas, make a list on the board of the different kinds of changes they mention. Possible ones are moving away, attending a different class or school, having an argument, changing one or both people's interests, and making new friends.

- Is it all right to lose or change friends? How do you feel when this happens?

Although children may share feelings of hurt and sorrow, share with them that all our friendships are constantly changing. Some are deepening; some are becoming more distant. Tell children that change in friendship is natural, and they will probably lose friends and establish new relationships throughout their lives.

- Have you ever heard this saying, *Make new friends, but keep the old. One is silver, and the other gold*? What do you think this means?

You may need to tell children that gold is more valuable than silver. Our old friends are more precious because we have shared more experiences with them. We have built trust and love over time. Usually old friends understand and care for us more than a new friend could.

Children can draw the different scenes from *The Giving Tree* on a large folded paper. They could also make up their own story in words or pictures of *A Changing Friendship.*

Use the illustration on p.175 for children to make a drawing or a collage of *The Giving Me.* They can draw themselves and then draw or find magazine pictures to illustrate the many things they could give. Encourage them to include skills they have and ways of helping and sharing as well as tangible items.

After the art project is complete, give children a homework assignment to actually give something they have pictured on their paper to someone. Have them share their feelings and experiences the next day.

A math-related activity that illuminates values about gift giving and receiving is creating friendship graphs. Make a copy of p.194 for each child to color and cut apart. Have children choose pictures to show which gifts they would most like to give and receive. Then make two graphs on butcher paper. Label one graph *Giving* and the other *Receiving*. Have the children glue the pictures of their favorite gifts to give and receive in the appropriate columns on the graphs (see p.195). With young children you can use the graphs to learn about the concepts of least, most, and the same, as well as to compute simple addition and subtraction problems. How many people wanted to receive either ice cream cones or hugs? How many fewer people wanted to give hugs than smiles? It is important with this activity not to make value judgments about what the children choose.

Give your children the opportunity to develop their creative skills by designing *The Ultimate Gift.* It could be painted, drawn, or built as a model using toothpicks, straws, clay, bottle caps, and other odds and ends.

Many of us have (or have had) a special tree in our yard or neighborhood that we climb, hug, or simply enjoy. Have children create stories and drawings of their real or imagined special trees. Set up a bulletin board display where they can post their work entitled *A Tree To Be Loved.*

PROBLEM SOLVING WITH CHILDREN'S BOOKS

Children's books on friendship also help children develop insight into their personal difficulties in relating to others. If you have a child with a problem or concern similar to one in a book, reading the book together is a simple way to open up a discussion.

When the problem discussed is thought to belong to the characters in the story, it is sometimes easier to share one's feelings. Solutions to the problem may reveal themselves in this nonthreatening atmosphere. Later on you could discuss privately with a child how some of the ideas and feelings shared about the story could help with the child's own problem.

The technique of using books to help children solve their problems and become aware of social concerns has been recently called *bibliotherapy,* but this practice has existed since books were first printed. *Healing place of the soul* was inscribed on the ancient library at Thebes. In the 1920s, bibliotherapy was first used by the medical profession. Since the 1940s, teachers and librarians have also adopted the practice to help children with their problems.

To be effective, bibliotherapy must not be forced. Setting up a book exhibit on a given theme encourages children to explore books on their own. You can also read the books at storytime and invite the children to discuss them afterward. Try to be sensitive to children's reactions. Encourage them to identify with the characters in the story and question their motives and actions. "What would you do if you were . . . ?" "Why do you think . . . acted that way?"

When we value children's opinions and responses we encourage them to develop new attitudes and behaviors. As children identify with the characters in the story, they may develop insights about how they can change their own lives.

Resources beginning on p. 210 contains an annotated list of books for primary children about the joys and problems of friendship. Also, additional activities and questions to use with two other books are found in Chapter 12, Our Human Family, on p.136. The children in your classroom will enjoy these stories as well as the lessons on friendship they have to offer.

THE FRIENDSHIP TREE 10

Friendship is a thing most necessary to life, since without friends no one would choose to live, though possessed of all other advantages.
—Aristotle

The Friendship Tree was developed for kindergarten and first grade children. I wrote the play to combine friendship studies with young children's natural interest in animals.

The play works well with a cast of anywhere from ten to thirty children. There are three principal roles: the Friendship Tree, the Flower Fairy, and the Mouse. The other woodland animal characters are on stage singing and dancing much of the time, but most have only one small speaking part each.

After you have chosen the main characters according to children's ability and interest, allow the other children to choose whichever forest creature they wish to be. Have children practice moving like their characters. It will be easier but not necessary to have two or three of each kind of creature, rather than all different ones.

Before you start rehearsals, make sure you and the children are familiar with the three songs and have developed tunes, dances, and hand movements as necessary. The school music teacher might enjoy helping with this aspect of the play.

The speaking parts in the play are provided as suggestions. Have the children make up their own lines and develop their creativity in the process. Children will also enjoy designing the set. Our set included a simple painted backdrop of a forest scene. Parents can help with making simple costumes and painting faces before the performance.

You or some other adult will probably want to be the narrator. You will also need to have an aide or parent to be your backstage helper to pull the curtain and cue the children. As the play begins, the children are standing with their partners in their assigned spots on the stage. The Friendship Tree is seated on a tall stool in the middle of the stage and stays there throughout the play.

(CURTAIN CLOSED)

NARR: Long ago, in a faraway land, there was a magical forest. It was here that creatures of all kinds could live together peacefully, with the help of the Friendship Tree. Blooming through all seasons, the Friendship Tree bestowed love and kindness on all living things and they shared the tree's happiness.

(CURTAIN OPENS)

(All forest creatures dance and sing the following with a partner. The tune to "Lord of the Dance" works well.)

I have friends in the forest, I have friends in the trees,
I have friends who fly on a gentle summer breeze,
and I know that you always will be my friend
in a special way that will never end.

(All forest creatures exit happily hand in hand behind the wing.)

NARR: Of course every now and then some of the creatures would have a disagreement, but the Friendship Tree had a marvelous way of warming their hearts and bringing kindness to their lives.

(The Flower Fairy and a bee enter arguing.)

FAIRY: You're always bugging me. Go away.

BEE: Bzzzz. But I like you.

FAIRY: Leave me alone!

FRIENDSHIP TREE: Let's be kind.

(The Friendship Tree sings this song using hand movements. The Flower Fairy and the bee watch and listen.)

> Kind hearts are the gardens, 🎵
> Kind words are the roots,
> Kind deeds are the flowers,
> Kind love is the fruit.

(The bee and Flower Fairy sing with the Friendship Tree and then all the others come back on stage with their partners and sing the song together.)

(CURTAIN CLOSES)

(Children sit down quietly where they were standing.)

NARR: My friends, I wish that our story could end here, with everyone living happily ever after, but life doesn't always work that way, and it didn't here in our magical forest. One day, in late fall, without warning, the Friendship Tree became ill.

(CURTAINS OPEN)

(The Friendship Tree is sick, coughing and sneezing.)

DEER: Oh, no, the Friendship Tree is sick!

BEAR: What can we do?

NARR: The wolves and coyotes had an idea.

WOLVES and COYOTES: We could howl for the Friendship Tree.

(Each time an idea is offered the others scoff at it, saying "oh no . . . forget it. . . that won't work . . ." and so forth.)

NARR: The rabbits and deer had an idea.

RABBITS and DEER: We could leap for the Friendship Tree.

NARR: The bears had an idea.

BEARS: We could growl for the Friendship Tree.

NARR: The birds, butterflies, and flowers had an idea.

BIRDS, BUTTERFLIES, and FLOWERS: We could show the Friendship Tree our colors.

NARR: And the friendly Flower Fairy had an idea.

FAIRY: We could be friends around the Friendship Tree.

(After the Flower Fairy's idea is rejected, she sadly goes and sits by herself at the edge of the stage. When she sits down the others start quietly arguing. "My idea would have worked" . . ."They had a silly idea" . . . and so forth.)

NARR: Oh, they just couldn't agree.

(The children need to listen for this cue to stop arguing. All the forest creatures stand and sing the following song to the tune of "Twinkle, Twinkle, Little Star.")

How can we help our Friendship Tree? ♫
It seems that we cannot agree.
You say do and I say don't.
I say will and you say won't.
How can we help our Friendship Tree?
It seems that we cannot agree.

(CURTAIN CLOSES)

(Children sit down in their places.)

NARR: With each passing day the forest creatures continued to argue and fight. This deeply saddened the Friendship Tree, whose health continued to fail. The tree began to wither and slowly die. It no longer had the energy to sing to cheer up the others. The magical forest became a dreary place to live.

(CURTAIN OPENS)

(The children all look sad. The Friendship Tree looks sad and ill.)

FAIRY: I don't want to live here anymore. Everyone is mean and nasty. Doesn't anyone want to be friends? Please? Can I be your friend? I want to be your friend.

(As the Flower Fairy goes around appealing to different characters, they each say no and walk off stage until the Fairy is alone. The Flower Fairy then sits down quietly at the foot of the seemingly dead Friendship Tree.)

(Mouse enters timidly.)

MOUSE *(softly):* I - I would like to be your friend.

FAIRY: What?

MOUSE *(louder):* I will be your friend.

FAIRY: Oh! You will? Say, do you remember that song the Friendship Tree taught us?

MOUSE: Yes, I think so. Let's try it.

(They sing and dance the "I have friends in the forest" song. The Friendship Tree moves a little and sighs.)

FAIRY *(to the tree):* Was that you? *(to Mouse)* Let's try it again.

(They sing and dance again and the Friendship Tree moves a little more and smiles weakly. The Flower Fairy and the Mouse go and get all the others who follow them on stage.)

FAIRY: Help us! We've found a way to cure the Friendship Tree!

(Everyone goes with a partner to their spots and sings "I have friends in the forest . . ." By the time they have finished singing, the Friendship Tree is sitting up, smiling, and looking healthy.)

NARR: As the forest creatures restored their friendship and kindness to one another, the Friendship Tree grew healthy and strong. The magic of love had returned to the forest and they all lived happily for the rest of their lives.

THE END

SECTION III

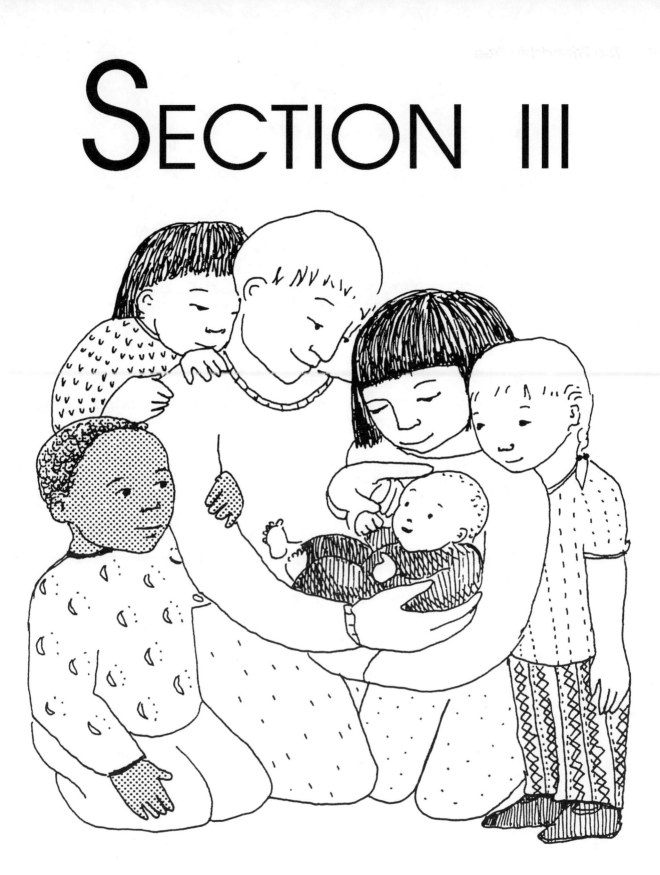

FOR THE WORLD

A WORLD OF FRIENDS 11

There is in friendship something of all relations, and something above them all. It is the golden thread that ties the heart of all the world.
—John Evelyn

Children today are growing up in a rapidly changing and interdependent world. Our food, clothes, cars, information, and household items travel to us from many parts of the globe. Never in the history of humanity have we been so connected and dependent upon each other. This intertwining of our lives is making the *small world* concept more real every moment.

To make sense of and function effectively in our diverse society and the international system, our children will need to understand and appreciate all the peoples of the earth. Many business and service sector jobs will require knowledge of other cultures and languages. Most important, many of the critical problems facing us will be solved only with intercultural understanding and cooperation.

Pollution, acid rain, poverty, and racism transcend national boundaries. These are just a few of the many challenges our children will face in the future. We cannot afford to make others our enemies when our lives hang in the balance.

THE HUMAN FAMILY

One way to help children develop an attitude of appreciation and caring for the people of the world is to introduce the concept of the *human family*, of our *relatives* around the planet. Although international studies are often reserved for the secondary school level, laying foundations at the primary level is essential if we want children to realize that we are all part of one human culture.

It is important to balance an understanding of our similarities with an appreciation of individual and cultural differences. Young children are usually honest in discussing the many ways people look and act. Their hearts and minds are more open than adolescents' to learning about the similarities and to appreciating the differences they have with children from other races and cultures.

Special activities and experiences focusing on other cultures are exciting opportunities for young children. Yet even more important are the many small ways we can bring the world into our classroom every day. We need to pay attention to the textbooks, audiovisual materials, storybooks, and bulletin board displays we use to ensure they reflect a variety of races and ethnic groups. Planning for field trips and special visitors can also expose students to more diversity than they might otherwise experience.

Are you aware of how many children of different racial and ethnic groups attend your school? We must teach children about the minority cultures that exist in the classroom and in the school. Children grow up inadvertently learning racism and cultural stereotyping. We need to openly explore these hidden attitudes and ideas, as well as to assist children in celebrating our diversity.

Children's parents are often more than willing to help with these efforts, which they realize are critical to their child's self-esteem and ability to make friends. If you have children in your classroom from different racial or ethnic groups, encourage parental involvement in the classroom. Parents are often the best source to learn about different cultural values, family dynamics, and special holiday celebrations.

In a school where other cultures are not well represented, the task of exposing children to cultural diversity requires more thought but is no less crucial. Young children need to know that many people in the world look, speak, and act differently than they do and yet are similar in countless other ways. The activities in the following chapters will help children extend their notion of family to other races and cultures around the world.

12 OUR HUMAN FAMILY

Not chance of birth or place has made us friends, Being often times of different tongues and nations, But the endeavor for the selfsame ends, With the same hopes, and fears, and aspirations.

—Henry Wadsworth Longfellow

ONE PEOPLE

Learning about people from other cultures often reveals the differences between us. If children are to see humanity as one people, we must also focus on our similarities. The following activities engage children in exploring the shared activities, abilities, needs, and desires of people around the world.

126

ACTIVITIES

One People

Skills: cooperation, communication, creative and critical thinking
Qualities: appreciation, understanding
Subjects: social studies, language arts, art

First, take some time to let children discover the meaning of the words *people* and *culture*, two words that you will use often in other activities. Ask the children how people are different from plants and animals.

On the board, write the words *look, think, feel, act*. Have the children first brainstorm the ways that humans look, think, feel, and act. For example, your lists might look something like this:

Look	Think	Feel	Act
nose	solve problems	happy	walk
two eyes	ask questions	sad	run
two ears	do puzzles	angry	sit
hands	read	confused	sleep
legs	write	proud	build
wear clothes	have ideas	hurt	talk

At first accept all the ideas children offer. Then go back and discuss them. Do all people wear clothes? Can everyone run? Although there are probably exceptions to almost all of the above characteristics, the lists point out some basic generalizations we can make about human beings:

- Most of us have bodies that are basically built the same (head, arms, ears) and that work in the same ways (walk upright, sit, sleep, use our hands to eat).
- We all experience a range of feelings.
- We use our minds to think, make decisions, and act.

Have the children discuss or draw how they do these things.

Children may want to talk about how many other animals share some of the characteristics in the lists. However, a human being is the only animal that fits all these descriptions. The important point here is that regardless of the differences between us (which the children will learn about and celebrate later in this chapter), we are all humans and in many ways, we are all the same.

This activity leads directly into the definition of *culture*. Rather than talking about different cultures, at this point define culture as the way of life unique to human beings. Children may want to discuss further some of the wonderful things that only humans can do such as build a model, plan and cook a meal, operate a computer, or grow a vegetable garden. Have children each share one thing that they can do that an animal or plant cannot do.

Find magazine pictures of adults and children from different cultures. Discuss differences in skin colors, hairstyles, dress, customs, housing, and so forth. What do we all have in common? At first children may feel there are more differences among us than similarities. Emphasize that all people share:

- a need for healthy food, clean water, and shelter
- the need to be safe
- a desire to enjoy life and be happy
- a need for love and belonging
- a desire to take good care of their children
- a desire to do meaningful, enjoyable work

Ask the children if they have these needs and desires. Do they like to feel safe? Do they need food and water every day? Does everyone in the room live in some kind of shelter to protect him or her from the weather?

In small groups, have children create an *earth collage* by pasting the cutout magazine pictures on a large paper circle. Children will need to cooperate so that everyone has some space for his or her picture. You might also want to copy the children's school pictures and include them in the collage.

CULTURE CONTACTS

The best way for children to develop an appreciation of people from other cultures is through direct experience. You may not be able to afford to take all the children to visit another country or ethnic community (although it is wonderful if you can). Following are some other ways that you can begin to build bridges of understanding.

A C T I V I T I E S

Culture Contacts

Skills: communication, cooperation, critical and creative thinking
Qualities: appreciation, understanding
Subjects: social studies, language arts, art

Seek out international visitors or students attending local colleges who would be willing to come to your classroom and talk about the ways of life in their countries. Other people may have recently moved to your community. Encourage them to share pictures, slides, and objects with your class as well as to talk about the lives of young children in their cultures.

For a cultural *show and tell,* invite a parent or member of your community who has lived in another country to come to class and talk about the culture. Ask them to give a hands-on, visual presentation if possible. Request that they focus on the similarities as well as the differences between cultures.

Provide an opportunity for children to share with children in another country or ethnic community through correspondence or media exchanges. Young children could help you write a group story or letter to be accompanied by individual drawings. Children could collect or make items that represent our culture to send to their new friends.

Subscribe to and submit writings and drawings to *Skipping Stones—A Multi-ethnic Children's Forum.* This quarterly journal is a compendium of children's poems, stories, artwork, riddles, and pen pal requests from all over the world. Many of the stories are printed in English as well as in the native language of the author. Each issue includes questions and ideas to prompt children's submissions. *Skipping Stones* is a "non-profit children's magazine to encourage co-operation, creativity, and celebration of cultural and linguistic diversity" that offers itself as a forum for communication among children from different lands and backgrounds. See *Resources* on p. 208 for subscription information.

MAKE-BELIEVE TRAVEL

Plan a pretend trip to a foreign country! If there are children from different cultures in your class, you might choose a country that will help all the children learn about that culture. For example, if you have Hispanic children in your class, choose a Spanish-speaking country in Central or South America. This make-believe adventure can be made exciting through many activities.

ACTIVITIES

Make-Believe Travel

Skills: communication, cooperation, creative thinking

Qualities: appreciation, understanding, tolerance

Subjects: social studies, language arts, art, mathematics

Make travel arrangements and plot your journey on the world map.

Have children make passports that include their pictures. (Use copied school pictures or other photographs.)

Learn about customs and climate so you'll know what to pack. Children can pack their suitcases by using the handout on p. 196. Make two copies of this sheet for each child. They can cut out pictures or draw the clothes and items they want to take with them. After the children cut out the suitcases, staple or tape the bottoms together so they can open up the suitcase to the contents inside.

Find out what you will be eating in the new country. Plan and prepare a common dish to get your stomachs ready.

Do you need any shots? What about the appropriate currency? Let children take turns being travelers, nurses, and bankers in role playing these situations.

Help children learn a few basic phrases in the new language.

Decide what you'll do when you get there and what cities and sites you'll visit. How will you share and interact with the local people to get to know them better?

A fitting culmination to these events will involve the help of parents or older students. Keep this part of the activity a surprise. Surprise the children one day by saying, "You have all spent so much time planning our trip, today we are going there!"

Going there happens when you walk with the children (and their suitcases and passports) to another room in the building where parents or upper grade students are ready for your visit. Arrange stations around the room that children can visit. Some of the many possibilities are:

- **Customs -** Suitcases are checked for any illegal items.
- **Passport Station -** Passports are checked and stamped.
- **Restaurant -** Foods are purchased in the language of the country. Children can also use foreign currency if you draw some on dittos and distribute it.
- **New Friends -** At this station have someone who will speak only the country's language. Children can use tourist phrases, nonverbal behavior, and sign language to try to communicate. If the children can read, you could also place some pocket dictionaries at this station.

Our Human Family ❖

- **Family Life** - At this station a few older students and two parents could role play a skit that shows some of the values and activities in family life.
- **Sight-seeing** - Use a number of stations where the children learn about cities and special attractions that you have talked about. An excellent research project for older children would be to prepare and give a presentation on one of the cities or tourist attractions in the country you are visiting. Another possibility for a station of this kind is to line up chairs as though they are on a bus and have a tour guide show the children around the country using a slide show or video display for visual effect.
- **Craft Shop** - This is another excellent project for older children, who can create a variety of crafts that are representative of those made in the country that you are visiting. The children can buy them with their dittoed currency or just observe them as museum pieces.

Depending on the number of children in the class and their maturity, you may want to organize this event in different ways. Stations could be color coded and matching tickets given out so that each child can visit each station only once. You could also place the children in groups and rotate them through the stations. If the children can handle it, however, they will have the most fun if they can roam freely from station to station.

PEOPLE

A special book filled with fascinating information about the similarities and differences among people around the world is the book *People* by Peter Spier. My class and I have so enjoyed this book that I am including here a wide variety of questions, discussion topics, and activities you can use along with reading it.

People

Skills: communication, cooperation, critical and creative thinking
Qualities: appreciation, understanding, tolerance
Subjects: social studies, language arts, art, physical education, mathematics

(pp. 1 and 2) The statistics may be interesting to you, but young children will probably not be able to make sense of them. Make sure you read the last two sentences.

(pp. 3 to 6) Have the children talk about and compare skin colors, heights, colors of eyes, noses, hairstyles, and so forth. Emphasize the wonder and beauty in diversity. Look at all the different ways babies are being carried on p. 3. Have children bring in their baby pictures to share.

(p. 7) Create a learning center with pictures of international clothing styles and a box of fabric pieces in assorted sizes and colors. Children can dress themselves in turbans, shawls, and robes. Have some belts or cord they can use to hold their costumes in place. Avoid stereotyping by emphasizing to children that in many cultures *traditional* clothing is worn only for special celebrations.

(p. 8) Discuss how what we consider beautiful has to do with our own point of view. Our perspective is influenced by where we grow up, what our parents and friends think, and things we see on television, as well as by other factors.

(p. 9) Children may be curious about the pictures and the stories behind them. Lessons or discussions on rules, laws, and safety would fit well here.

(p. 10) Have children draw pictures of *A Noise I Love* and *My Idea of a Good Time*. They can dictate or write sentences to describe their pictures. The drawings could then be assembled into class books.

(pp. 11 and 12) Have children guess how some of the games are played. How many have they heard of? Some of the games, like Yobuzimo and Sukatan, can easily be played in the classroom. You might also want to introduce the children to the concept of cooperative games. See books and companies for buying cooperative games listed in *Resources* on pp. 203 and 204.

❀

(pp. 13 and 14) Discuss why people's houses are so different. Consider climate, availability of resources, economics, reflection of family or community values, and lifestyles. Set up a learning center where children can design their own homes or build homes that resemble those in the book. Materials could include:

- basic art supplies (scissors, paints, crayons, paper)
- small, clean milk cartons (for a typical suburban home)
- clay (for mud huts, castle walls)
- fabric scraps (for tents, teepees, village homes)
- toothpicks (for homes on stilts or roofs)
- raffia (for grass roofs)
- Lego's small building blocks (for brick homes, castles)
- sticks (for teepee supports, log homes)

Collect more books on different types of housing for children to look at while they create their own. Try not to specify a particular home children should all make. Allow their creativity and imagination to flourish instead.

🍎

Assemble all the homes in one area of the room or on a large board as a *global village*. This activity could also be extended by having children use little play people to live in the homes and interact with each other. Here are some ideas for role playing:

- Have people visit each other's homes and learn about how and why they were designed the way they were.
- Give the children a common problem such as overpopulation, lack of food, or scarcity of fuel for heating and cooking. Have the little global villagers meet and try to solve the problem together.

- Have the children learn about a custom of the culture in which their home is based. The little global people could visit each other's homes and learn about the customs.
- Free play. Children will create their own wonderful scenes and problems.

(pp. 15 and 16) Ask children to relate the ideas on these pages to their personal experience. What makes them laugh or cry? Is there something they do especially well? Ask them to tell the class about something they like to do alone and something they like to do with others.

(pp. 17 and 18) Make a graph of the pets the children own (see diagram below). See Chapter 8, *Friendly Holidays,* for ideas on celebrating the Chinese New Year.

🐹	🐟	🐶	🐍	🐱	🐢
George		Tom		Mira	Sue
		Chan	Ty		Leroy
	Marta			Julio	

(pp. 19 and 20) Isn't it amazing that there are so many foods in the world? Bring in some new and unusual foods for the children to try. Some possibilities are dates, figs, tahini, kiwi fruit, papaya, or plaintain. Most of these are available at a local grocery store.

(pp. 21 and 22) These ideas may be too abstract for young children. Some children may be fascinated by the differences in the statues or houses of worship.

(pp. 23 and 24) Ask the children to tell you which of the jobs on page 23 they would like to have and why. Share with them how doing a job well is a way of helping others.

(pp. 25 and 26) Learning sign language is a fun activity. You can also teach the children some simple phrases and words in another language and then use them from time to time in the classroom. Below are some Spanish phrases you could use. I have chosen Spanish because so many of our neighbors to the south speak this language and the Hispanic population in our country is growing.

How are you?	Como estan ustedes?
Fine, thank you.	Bien, gracias.
Let's line up.	Vamos a ponernos en fila.
Who is ready to play?	Quien esta lista para jugar?
Come in.	Entren ustedes.
lunch time	hora de almorzar
please	por favor
good job	bien hecho
good-bye	adios

If young children are exposed to other languages in their early school years, they will be less likely to feel that the words and the people who speak them are strange.

(pp. 27 and 28) Children may want to try writing letters or numbers in another language. An excellent book for young children that introduces them to the numbers one through ten in Japanese is *Count Your Way Through Japan* by Jim Haskins.

(pp. 29 and 30) What is power? Who are the people in your school, community, and country who have power? If children think of power solely as physical strength, introduce the idea of power as using one's intellect and social skills to make changes in life.

(pp. 31 and 32) The content on these two pages may be too abstract for the children. Follow their lead on whether they find these examples interesting.

(pp. 33 and 34) One example you can use to point out that people look and dress the way they do for good reasons are the Bedouins, a nomadic people living in the Sahara Desert. At first it might seem strange that these people live in tents and wear long robes and scarves on their heads and faces. Describe their environment—hot, sunny, windy, dry—and their lifestyle—traveling with animal herds searching for water—and see if the children can tell you why the Bedouins dress and live so differently than we. Emphasize to the children that if they were Bedouins, they would dress and live in these natural and useful ways.

(pp. 35 to 38) These pages illustrate the richness of diversity. Have the children look for other languages and international influences on pages 37 and 38.

I recommend that you savor this book slowly with the children. Leave it out for them as they will want to look at it again and again.

Miss Rumphius

A book that celebrates the diversity in the world and our responsibility to make the world more beautiful is *Miss Rumphius* by Barbara Cooney. In this delightfully illustrated book, we follow the life of Miss Rumphius from her childhood, influenced by her well-traveled artist grandfather, to her own journey to foreign lands and then finally to her life by the sea where she learns to give something back to the earth. Following are some ideas for sharing this book with the children in your class.

A C T I V I T I E S

Miss Rumphius

Skills: communication, creativity
Qualities: appreciation, understanding
Subjects: language arts, art

What kinds of stories do you think Alice's grandfather tells her? Have the children make up a group story about adventures in faraway places. One child says a sentence or two to begin the tale and then other children add on parts. The story builds and grows as it moves among the children.

Share some folktales with the children that illustrate the customs and cultures in which the stories originated. Do any of these stories make them feel like traveling to faraway places?

How did Miss Rumphius become friends with the Bapa Raja? Do they think she thought the Bapa Raja was strange? Why or why not? Although this scene is related simply in the book, there is a wonderful feeling of mutual respect and appreciation.

Miss Rumphius chooses planting fields of lovely lupine flowers as her way of making the world more beautiful. Have the children brainstorm other ways to make the earth a better place for us all to live. Caring for the earth, our life support system, and its people is the greatest act of friendship we can offer our human family. Have the children draw or paint their favorite way of making the world more beautiful.

13 FRIENDSHIP QUILT PROJECT

Friendship improves happiness, and abates misery, by doubling our joy, and dividing our grief.
—Joseph Addison

In spring 1983 my kindergarten class made a quilt to promote world friendship and peace. In our initial discussion of the project, one little boy was shocked to hear that we would send the quilt to children in the Soviet Union. "My daddy says they're bad and when I grow up I'm gonna shoot them in a war," he pronounced. I explained that most Soviets, like most Americans, were nice and wanted to be peaceful and that some Russians think we're bad, too. At this the children laughed and cried "they must be dumb 'cause we're nice." As I continued to explain the situation, I found that most of the children were able to see that fear and ignorance has caused us all to be a little dumb.

The quilt project is a wonderful way to begin breaking through the barriers of fear and misinformation and to develop friendships with real people in other countries. I received a picture of the quilt being presented to the Women's Peace Committee in Moscow, and local newspapers covered the event both here

144

and in Moscow. My class received two packages of letters, drawings, and other gifts from the school children who put our quilt on display in their school. Smiles were abundant, hearts were warmed in both countries, and the children learned that friendly people live in many parts of the world.

Below is part of a letter and a drawing that my children received from the Soviet Union.

We can tell you many interesting things about our contry and Moscow. We want to invi-te you to come to Moscow and see that we are not so "bad" as some of you think.

PLANNING THE PROJECT

You can integrate making a quilt with the rest of your curriculum in many ways. We made the quilt while studying the letter "Q," displayed it at our annual art show, and used animals as our theme when we were doing a unit on animals. If you plan to teach a unit on friendship, peace, or world cultures, the quilt project is obviously an ideal centerpiece.

The quilt project can be simple or complex, depending on the needs and interests of your class. You can adjust the size of the quilt to accommodate the number of children in the class. Making a friendship quilt can be a month-long project or a simple afternoon's activity. Read through the rest of this chapter to learn about different possible quilting methods. Then fill in the information on the following page. This process will help you design a project that will suit your needs.

Designing a Quilting Project

Grade_____   Number of children_____

Length of time you want to spend on:

    Planning and introductory activities_____

    Quilt making_____

    Follow-up activities_____

Availability of extra help:

    Parent volunteers_____

    Older students_____

    Senior citizens_____

    Other_____

Amount of time you have to spend_____

Ideas for funding sources (P.T.A., parents, fundraising event)

Other units with which you would like to combine this project

Talk with the children about your ideas. Encourage dialogue and questions about the project. If possible, share news of similar projects carried out in other schools. Another way to get your children excited about quilt making is to read them one of the children's books in *Resources* on p. 209.

Increase your children's excitement by having them make decisions about the project. They may enjoy choosing the theme or the quilting method. Ask the children if they would like to exhibit the finished quilt at school or in a local library or post office before giving it away.

Children can also discuss whom they would like to receive the quilt. We sent ours to another school. In the Soviet Union, youth groups, children's hospital wards, and orphanages are a few of the many possibilities.

Collect the necessary materials, set up a time to brief extra helpers if any are involved, and you are ready to start!

METHODS

There are many ways to make a quilt. Many of the following methods do not require any sewing by the children. The general instructions that follow should be used with any technique.

1. The quilt squares can range in size from 9" to 12" depending on how many squares you have. For 12 squares in a quilt, squares can be 12" by 12". If you plan to put 24 or 25 squares in a quilt, make them 9" or 10" square.

2. Decide whether children will be painting, drawing, or sewing on the material, then check the material for the suitability of the chosen method. Best to use is 100 percent cotton. Make sure you wash it first because it will shrink.

3. Always have children sketch their picture or design on scrap paper first. It will be easier for the children to copy the design on the material if the drawings are done to scale.

4. If possible, allow the children a practice session with the chosen methods and material. The final product will be better executed if children can experiment first. The following methods are listed from the simplest to the more complex.

Fabric Markers

Grades: K-6
Time: 1 hour
Materials: fabric squares, fabric markers or needle-point pens
Extra help: none

Children draw their pictures in pencil and fill in with markers over the sketch.

Acrylic Painting

Grades: K-6
Time: 1 hour
Materials: fabric squares, brushes, acrylic paints
Extra help: none or one adult

Children draw their picture in pencil on a fabric square, then paint over the sketch. If the drawing is done on dark material, use a white pencil. The finished quilt can be hand-washed gently if necessary. You can also use fabric paints.

Fabric Crayons

Grades: K-6
Time: 1 hour
Materials: fabric squares, fabric crayons, paper, iron, ironing board
Extra help: one adult

Crayola makes special crayons that can be ironed into fabric. Children can draw on paper with fabric crayons. The paper is placed on the fabric square and ironed. (Note that words must be drawn backwards to come out correctly on the fabric.) Complete directions are on the package. This is my favorite technique, especially for young children.

Fabric Markers and Sewing

Grades: K-6
Time: 3 one-hour sessions
Materials: fabric squares, fabric markers, yarn or embroidery thread, large needles
Extra help: an older student or adult for each young child

Children sketch their designs on the fabric square in pencil. Then they outline the picture with markers and sew a running stitch on top of the outline. Parts of the design can be colored in with markers.

Drawing and Sewing

Grades: K-6
Time: children-1 hour, adults-1 to 10 hours
Materials: fabric squares, embroidery thread, needles
Extra help: adults

Children draw a picture on paper or the square itself. Adults sew and embroider the children's designs. This method allows for only a small contribution from the children, but you will have a nice finished product.

Cut-Out Shapes

Grades: 2-6
Time: 2 to 10 hours
Materials: fabric squares, felt, needles, thread
Extra help: none

Children draw a picture on the square itself, then cut out felt shapes for the picture. Children sew the shapes to the fabric squares. (Note that this quilt will not be washable. The felt would run.)

ASSEMBLING THE QUILT

Here are the dimensions for a 24-square quilt using the lattice method.

Lattice material: (2" wide strips) 2 yards of 44/45" fabric (can be done with less if you want to put a seam in the middle of the lengthwise lattice strips)

Backing material: 2 yards of 44/45" fabric (one seam in the middle of the backing)

Squares: $1\frac{2}{3}$ yards of 44/45" fabric (cut squares 10" by 10")

The directions that follow can be used to assemble the quilt squares. The assembling will need to be done by adults. If possible, have the children watch some of the process so they can see what happens after their squares are done.

Sewing the Quilt Top Together

Make sure all the squares are the same size. Arrange the squares into rows, preferably forming a rectangle.

Method 1: Machine sew the squares together. Machine sew bias tape, rick-rack, ribbon, or other trim between the squares.

Method 2: Lattice method. You'll need fabric to sew between the squares. A solid color will show the squares off best (fig. A). Decide how wide you would like the lattice between the squares. Cut one-half inch wider, allowing for a one-quarter-inch seam. Add the quilt square measurements and the lattice measurements and cut long strips for each side length between the rows (fig. B). Cut short strips the same length as your quilt squares for the remainder (fig. C). Sew the rows of quilt squares and lattice together (fig. C) with a one-quarter-inch seam. On the wrong side, iron seams toward the darkest fabric. Sew long lattice strips between rows and on edges. Press seams.

Some other notes: If you have squares left over after placing them in rows, use them as simple pillow covers. Leave them unstuffed for shipping. If you do not have enough squares, you can make up the difference by including message squares. The children can print a message of friendship or the name of the class and school on the fabric and an adult can embroider on top.

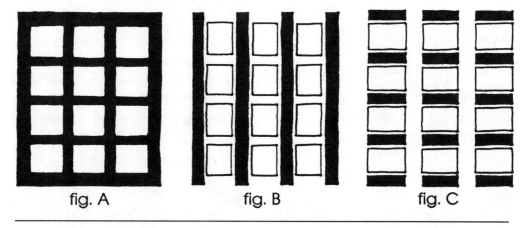

fig. A   fig. B   fig. C

Assembling Quilt Layers

You need batting for the inside. Commercial batting can be bought at a fabric store or you may use old lightweight washable blankets. Sheet blankets are fairly easy to find at a second-hand store. You will also need a backing. Cottons are best. Prewash if new. A color-coordinated print is nice for this.

Method 1: This method is the easiest. Cut all quilt layers the same size. Layer them in this order: backing (face down), batting, quilt top (face up). Smooth out and baste (fig. D). Machine sew strips of fabric, bias tape, decorative tape, or washable ribbon on top of the seams between the squares (fig. E). Finish the edges with bias tape.

Method 2: For a more professional look, try this method. The backing will be your largest fabric piece, as it will fold over to form the border. Lay the backing face down and smooth out. Then layer your batting and quilt top, smoothing each layer out flat (fig. F).

The batting will be the next largest piece depending on the border size you have chosen. Baste all layers together with a very large basting stitch (fig. D).

Sewing the Layers Together
(for Method 2 above)

Fold the backing over to the front side, over the batting, to the edge of the quilt top. Fold over one-quarter inch and pin or baste (fig. G). Fig. G shows two ways to fold the corners. Hand or machine stitch border edge to quilt top. Leave the basting in until you have completed the quilt.

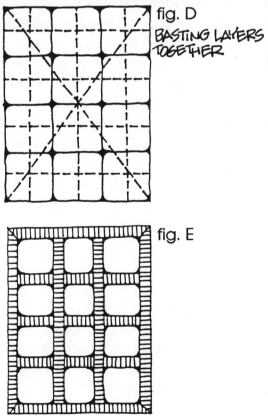

fig. D

BASTING LAYERS TOGETHER

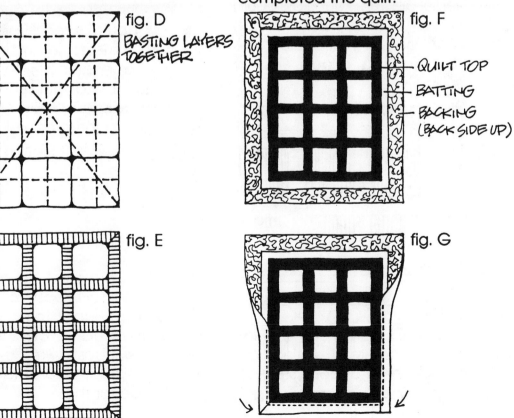

fig. F

QUILT TOP

BATTING

BACKING (BACK SIDE UP)

fig. E

fig. G

To secure the layers more firmly and to give a quilt look, use the following methods.

Method 1: This is the quickest and easiest way and also one in which the children can participate. You will need darning needles and colorful washable yarn. Stitch through all layers and tie in a bow or knot on the front of the quilt. See fig. H for suggested places to tie the yarn.

Method 2: Choose areas to machine stitch (fig. I).

Method 3: Have others help you quilt the layers. Parents might want to help or a local quilting group at a church or senior center. Your class could go on a field trip to watch them quilt or you could invite the quilting group to the school.

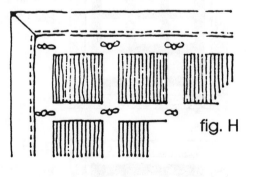

fig. H

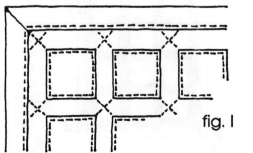

fig. I

FOLLOW-UP ACTIVITIES

- Have the students write a paragraph explaining each quilt square and include them with a diagram of the quilt, all to be sent along with the quilt.
- Have students write a page *About Me* to introduce themselves. They could include drawings or snapshots of themselves as well.
- Spread the good news! Get school newsletter or local newspaper coverage, maybe even a television spot. Display the quilt. Share this section on quilting with your colleagues.
- You could even tape record a message and send the tape along with the quilt. How about learning some Russian phrases and including them as well?

How TO GET QUILTS TO THE SOVIET UNION

Contact: The Sunbow Quilt Project
            c/o Betsy Bridwell
            3216 NE 103rd
            Seattle, WA 98125
            (206) 525-9569

The Sunbow Quilt Project is in touch with many groups and individuals visiting the Soviet Union and possibly other countries. You will need to supply a compact carrying bag with a shoulder strap or handle for your Friendship Quilt. Each quilt deliverer is required to submit a written report and photographs of the quilt being presented to its recipients. You will receive this documentation after the quilt deliverer returns to the United States.

14 CHILD'S PLAY

*Do you carrot
all for me?
My heart
beets for you.
With your
turnip nose
And your
radish face,
You are a
peach.
Lettuce marry.
Weed make a
swell pear.*
—Children's
pun

The study of children's games and play around the world brings the ideas of interdependence and cross-cultural understanding into familiar territory for children. What young child does not like to spend hours engaged in some sort of play? Play is universal in all cultures, although it may look different depending on cultural norms and values. Much of children's play, however, is the same, no matter the country or the historical period.

Play is a rich and complex phenomenon. Play engages the whole person: mind, heart, and body. One can learn much about children through their play—their drives, desires, anxieties, and dreams. An individual and a social process, both at once, play can take many forms. One can watch children rehearse the roles and challenges of adult life, develop needed emotional and physical skills, and experiment with imagination, power, and sex roles.

In learning about games and play in many countries, young children will further develop their understanding of the similarities they share with other children. They can begin to transcend cultural barriers and learn to see distant people as their friends around the world.

As teachers we generally look at play as a recess activity, outside the context of important school lessons. When we realize the potential of play in children's development, both socially and individually, we may want to include play in the classroom as well.

Many types of children's play are universal. Games that use tag, hiding, dolls, balls, wheels, and singing are widespread. Some kinds of play seem developmental and occur in cultures all over the world, such as imitating adults and hiding. Other types of play originated in one part of the world and have traveled the globe, transmitted from one culture to another. Kite flying, which began in the Far East, is one example. It is in this kind of children's play that we can focus on interdependence. We depend on each other around the planet for many ideas, goods, and services. Games are one delightful component of our interconnection.

Descriptions of young children's play in countries around the world follow, along with discussion questions and activities for the children in your classroom.

Child's Play

Skills:	communication, cooperation, creative thinking
Qualities:	sharing, appreciation of diversity
Subjects:	physical education, language arts, art

PAPUA, NEW GUINEA

Many different types of children's play and games exist within each culture. One type of play for the children living at the ocean's edge in New Guinea involves balance games. Most of the homes are on stilts over

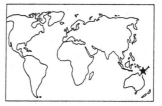

155

the water and the children need to climb ten-foot ladders as well as stand safely on their porches overlooking the surf. Balance is therefore a critical skill for the development of these children.

The girls play a game in which one child stands on a plank holding a balancing rod. Other children pick up the board and walk about to and fro as the child with the rod dances and sings. When she falls off, it is another girl's turn to stand on the plank.

In the boys' game, the boys stand in pairs facing each other and hold their arms to make a sort of human ladder, similar to our "firefighter's carry." One boy tries to walk across the arms of his friends without falling. After the walker has crossed the arms of one pair, they quickly run to the end of the line so the walker can keep going as long as his skill holds out. When he falls off, it is another boy's turn to try.

Discussion Questions

- Do these games sound hard for us to do? (Probably. Because of their lifestyle, the children in coastal Papua, New Guinea, must develop these skills early in life. Another interesting fact is that most of them learn to swim before they walk.)

- Why do you think the girls play different games than the boys? (Girls and boys in this culture have different roles to fulfill as adults. The boys need more balance skills than the girls because in their culture, the boys are the hunters. They must be able to throw a spear carefully while standing in a boat.)

- What kinds of balancing games do we play? (Think of the balance beam, walking on fences, standing on one foot. Most of our play at balancing is an individual feat.)

Activity

If children are interested, have them try a modified version of one of the games above. For the board game, first practice on a stationary board on the ground, then on a board supported by a log at either end. For the firefighter carry, have the children in double lines kneel on the ground. The walker might also try traversing the line kneeling at first rather than standing. Of course boys and girls can play both games. Emphasize to the children the importance of building their balance skills slowly and safely.

LIBERIA, AFRICA

Liberian children ages four through seven were observed in the following imitative play. One child was the "blacksmith," another the "client." The blacksmith used sticks, rocks, and bamboo pieces as tools to form a "machete" by hammering it and putting it in and out of the "fire." The machete was then given to the client to take into the "jungle" to cut brush.

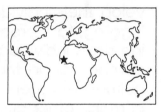

Discussion Questions

- Why do you think the children used sticks and stones, rather than real toys, in their play? (Most children in the world, including the children in Liberia, have few if any toys as we know them. Their parents must spend any available money on food, clothing, and housing.)

- Do you ever pretend to be someone else when you play? (Children may mention mom or dad while playing house or a superhero, cops and robbers, and so forth.)

Activity

Collect objects from outside such as small rocks, sticks, stones, pinecones, shells, nuts, and leaves. Have the children use these objects in free play or in creating skits they present to the class. Afterward, ask them how it felt to play with these " toys." (Note that some children will be readily able to imagine these objects as props in their play. Others will be so conditioned by commercial toys that they will find this extremely difficult.)

ESKIMOS, ALASKA

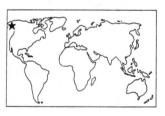

Eskimo children play many games that develop their individual skills. Dart throwing, juggling, tag, broad jumping, and foot racing stress individual betterment rather than competition in this cooperatively oriented culture. Another form of Eskimo play, found in many other cultures as well, is the creation of string figures. Many different patterns create forms that symbolize cultural aspects of Eskimo life.

Discussion Questions

- How many of the Eskimo games mentioned have you played?

- Have you ever played "cat's cradle"? (Cat's cradle is a simple string figure done on two hands.)

Activity

See p.186 for two simple string figures the children can try. *Resources* on p. 209 also lists books with other string figures interested children may want to learn.

BALI

The children of Bali play many games that develop physical skills by incorporating chasing and tagging. A number of the games designate one child as "it" while the other children run or hide. The following game is based on the mythical Bird Ga-Ga.

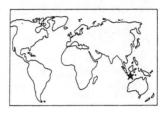

One child, playing the role of Bird Ga-Ga, sits in the middle of the group. Bird Ga-Ga closes his or her eyes and places the egg on the ground behind. One of the other players then steals the Bird's egg and hides it. Bird Ga-Ga then goes in search of the egg.

Discussion Questions

- How many games can you think of that involve running, chasing, tagging, or hiding? (The children should be able to come up with many games that include one or more of these elements.)

- Do we play games that have an "it"? What games does the Bird Ga-Ga game remind you of? (Hide-and-seek and Steal the Flag are two possibilities.)

Activity

Find an object that resembles an egg. A small ball will work well. Play the Bird Ga-Ga game as it is played in Bali. Perhaps the children would like to change the character in the game. Some possibilities could be a mother and baby or a firefighter and truck.

AUSTRALIA

Australian children enjoy creating their own patterns on which to hop and pick up rocks without losing their balance. They call these games *Hoppy.* On p.197 you will find some Hoppy patterns and their names.

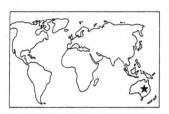

Discussion Questions

- What game that we play seems similar to Hoppy? (The children will think of hopscotch.)

- Do the Australian versions seem harder or easier than ours? (Most of the Australian versions involve more numbers and more complex patterns.)

Activity

Have the children draw on paper a Hoppy pattern they would like to try. It could be one from p.197 or a design of their own. Then go outside with a big piece of chalk and find a suitable area for drawing some of the Hoppy patterns. (Note that it may be difficult for young children to transfer their ideas from paper to asphalt in the appropriate size. An adult may be needed to carry out this part of the activity.)

!KUNG TRIBE, SOUTHWEST AFRICA

The children in the !Kung tribe play in many different ways. Like the children in many other cultures, they often create toys using natural and found objects, such as making a toy gun out of reed or making a car out of tubers and bulbs. Young girls make dolls out

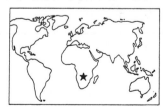

of clay, bananas, or ears of corn with braided rope hair. They may also build small huts for the dolls out of sand and twigs.

Discussion Questions

● The !Kung tribe children and many other children around the world have no toys. Why do you think this is so? (In most cases, the children would like to own toys and their parents would like to be able to buy them, but often there is not enough money to spend on toys and, in many rural areas, no shops or stores where toys are sold.)

● How do you think you would feel if you were a child who had no toys? What if you lived in a village where none of the children had toys? Would this make a difference? Although children will probably say they would be sad, angry, or bored, try to get them to see that they probably feel that way because they are used to having toys to play with and it would be a loss for them. Children in the !Kung tribe enjoy inventing toys and are mostly happy in their play and games.)

Activity

Collect natural items as well as scrap objects such as milk cartons, bottle caps, and tin cans. Provide string, wire, and nails to join the pieces together. Have the children make toys they think boys and girls in the !Kung tribe would enjoy playing with. Other useful objects for this project would be:

yarn	all the natural items from the
fabric scraps and trims	Liberian children's game
buttons	empty thread spools
wood scraps	Popsicle sticks
cardboard	straws
old socks	bananas
aluminum foil	stuffing

You may also want to show your children films listed in *Resources* on p. 210. The films briefly show children from other cultures at play. It is particularly interesting to compare *Debree's Playhouse*, a film of Vermont children building a treehouse, with *Baobab Play*, in which !Kung children play in a large tree.

The activities in this chapter only begin to explore the wonderful world of children's play and games. Our friends around the world have many more fascinating types of play that you and your children can learn about.

EVALUATING THE DEVELOPMENT OF FRIENDSHIP

To be capable of steady friendship and lasting love are the two greatest proofs, not only of goodness of heart, but of strength of mind.
—William Hazlitt

It is important to evaluate children's friendship skills. As teachers, we need to know if our efforts in the classroom are benefiting children, and we want to share with parents and administrators information about children's progress in their studies. However, the traditional methods of evaluation may not be appropriate to use with friendship studies.

Most teachers are trained to state the desired outcomes for a student's learning in measurable objectives. We then determine whether children have accomplished the prescribed tasks by giving them either teacher-made or standardized tests.

But *friendship* is not easily defined or always measurable. It is certainly not a list of items that we can test children on to see if they remember, nor is it a subject that can be mastered in a month-long unit or even in a year of studies. Friendship is a complex web of skills and qualities we all develop throughout our lives.

163

How then can we assess and share with others children's learning in this important subject? The principal tools available to us in this endeavor are interaction and observation. By interacting with children, we not only build healthy relationships but we also may observe the skills and qualities children manifest in relating to others. We also need to develop a keen eye. By watching children we can become aware of the skills and qualities of particular children that deserve more of our attention.

The charts on p.198 and p.199 may be used to record your assessment of children's friendship skills and qualities. The first list includes broad categories; the second provides more detail on specific behavior. These lists can be used in the following ways:

- to establish a beginning baseline assessment of children's abilities before beginning the study of friendship
- to record observations about a particular child and his or her progress
- to assess which skills and qualities the class as a whole needs to develop in their friendship studies
- to share with parents and administrators
- to record children's progress in weekly, monthly, or semester intervals
- to comment to the children on their progress, for example, "Tom, you have really learned to share with others this year!"

Through interaction and observation, and by recording our impressions, we can genuinely assess our children's development and share their progress with others.

CONCLUSION 16

The making of friends, who are real friends, is the best token we have of a (person's) success in life.
—Edward Everett Hale

The study and practice of friendship in the classroom will transform children, teachers, and schools. The atmosphere of joy and harmony that develops cannot be contained within four walls. It spills out into the teachers' room and onto the playground. Children take it home to their families and neighborhoods. Our efforts to create healthy relationships will have far-reaching effects that we will never know about.

Yet the deepest effect can be felt within ourselves. As we work on creating healthy attitudes and taking positive actions with children, we will discover greater warmth and less distance toward the little people we care about. We can relax more, feel more authentic, and share more fully in the learning that takes place. We can work with children rather than against them, apologize when we make mistakes, and share their joy when they succeed.

When we see the results of focusing on friendship, we may begin to question how we spend our hours in the classroom. Reading, writing, and arithmetic will always be important skills. But what do we read and write about? We can opt for themes that increase children's sense of appreciation for themselves and others. How much time do we spend memorizing facts? Will they be remembered five or ten years from now? Do we need to memorize so much when such information is so readily available through computers? In answering these questions, we may find even more time available for the study of friendship.

My goal in educating children has gradually shifted to include *being* as well as *doing*. I want the children in my class to *do* reading, writing, and math, but I also want to help them *be* the best people they can. My vision for each child is expressed clearly in the following:

> . . . the creation of a deeper, fuller human being, strong in body and full of mental brilliance; having a clear sense of Self; capable of childlike playfulness and joy; open to life's joys and sorrows; keenly sensitive to nuances of energy underlying the material world, and ultimately connected with all of humanity. A new type of human, one might almost say,—capable of creating an ever more humane, satisfying, meaningful world.
> —Dori Smith, *Whole Life Times*, Sept./Oct. 1982

Our schools have put much effort into pursuing academic excellence. It is time to put commensurate energy into promoting human excellence. Only when we begin to balance academic with social and emotional growth can we hope to create healthy people who can cope with the complexities of life. Only creative minds and caring hearts may help to heal our troubled world. Friendship is the journey of that caring and we can be the guides. Join hands with the children. Give the gift of friendship to yourself, your children, and your world!

Appendix
Blackline Masters and Resources

_____ is doing

Grrrreat!

_____
teacher

_____
had a great day today.
I enjoy having you in class.

168

_____
teacher

Oh NO! Not again!	Leave me alone.
You are amazing!	I can't believe it.
I want to be alone.	Please help me.
I did it all by myself.	Are you coming with me?
Why did you leave?	Look what you did!
Is something in the bushes?	I can't do it.
I'll never finish.	You're not very nice.
I'm having a party.	I won't play with you.
Pick up your toys!	I helped her finish.
You're not my friend.	Why are you always late?

messy room	broken toy
spilled milk	ripped book
lost coat	birthday present
muddy shoes	dirty shirt
tangled hair	new puppy
sleeping late	perfect paper
too noisy	big hello
friendly smile	lost ball
shared lunch	won't let me play
kicked leg	a big hug

Name_____

Directions: Create five "I messages" in the blanks at the bottom of the page by using the words in the boxes below.

When you...	I feel...	because...
come to school late	happy	you hurt their feelings
do your best	sad	you end up playing alone
hit other people	angry	I know you're having fun
won't share	annoyed	it interrupts our morning
smile	proud	you are learning so much

When you _____ I feel _____

because _____ .

When you _____ I feel _____

because _____ .

When you _____ I feel _____

because _____ .

When you _____ I feel _____

because _____ .

When you _____ I feel _____

because _____ .

With PARTNERS we . . .

1. SHARE ideas and materials.
2. LISTEN to each other.
3. SUPPORT each other by believing in and helping our partners.
4. Use quiet voices.
5. Stay in our seats.

We sink or swim together.

Two heads are better than one.

Partners' names _____ and _____

Underline the sentences that show SHARING or SUPPORT.

1. Wow, that's a great idea!
2. I had fun working with you today.
3. Let me do that! I can do it much better than you can.
4. Could you help me practice my spelling words?
5. That's a terrible idea.
6. Thanks for showing me how to do that problem.
7. I want to do it all!
8. Come on, you can do it!
9. Please hand me the scissors.
10. Don't be stupid. Try harder.
11. What a weird idea.
12. Can you explain how you got that answer?
13. I don't want to be your partner anymore.
14. We have a problem. Let's see if we can solve it.
15. What would you like to work on next?
16. I know we'll get it right if we keep trying.
17. I never thought about it that way. Maybe that will work.
18. I want to do it my way!

25 Ways to SUPPORT your partner when the answer is RIGHT . . .

1. Good job!
2. Great!
3. Wow!
4. Thanks!
5. Super!
6. Terrific!
7. Wonderful!
8. You got it!
9. Fantastic
10. Awesome!
11. Amazing!
12. All right!
13. Right on!
14. Give me five!
15. Out of sight!
16. Yea!
17. Ya!
18. Hurray!
19. Neat-o!
20. You're right!
21. Stupendous!
22. (Thumbs up)
23. (Okay)
24. (Shake hands)
25. (Smile)

and when the answer is WRONG . . .

1. Try again.
2. May I show you?
3. Think again.
4. Try another guess.
5. You can do it.
6. Look again.
7. Look carefully.
8. Let's try it this way.
9. Let's do another one.
10. Let's do this one again.
11. May I help you?
12. Better luck next time.
13. It's hard, isn't it?
14. Why do you think that?
15. No, try again.
16. Can you figure it out?
17. This may help.
18. Take a guess.
19. Come on, once more.
20. Here's what I think.
21. Look at this part.
22. You got this part right.
23. Here's how I would do it.
24. I know you're trying.
25. One more time.

174

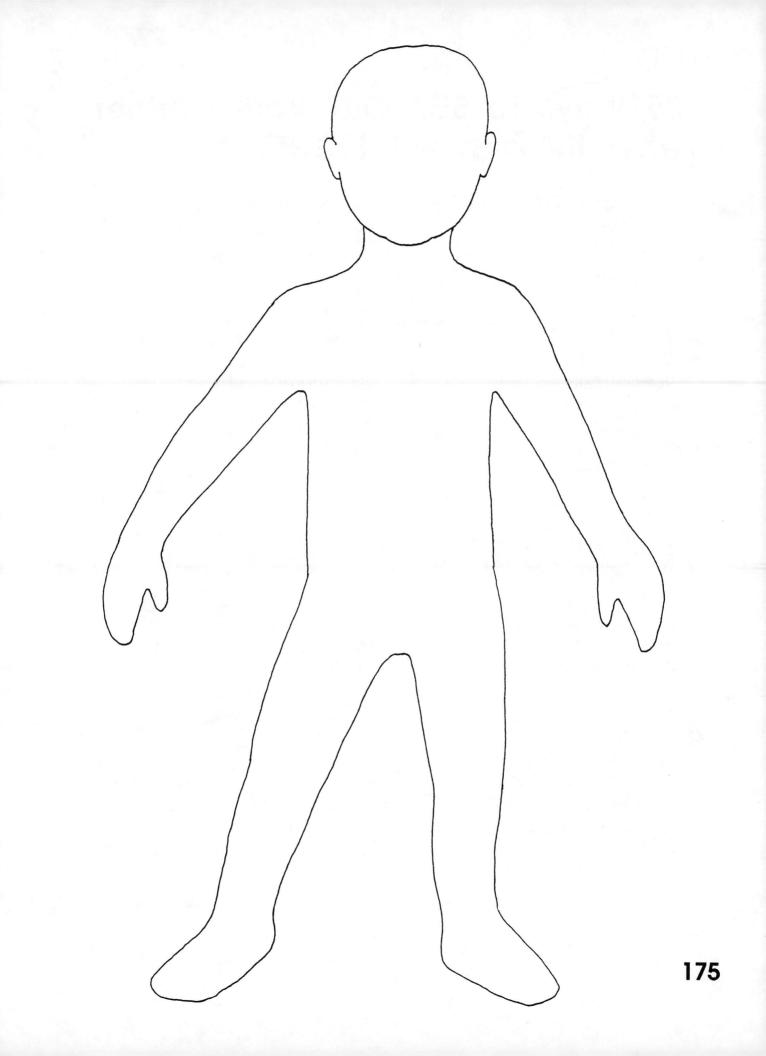

175

RED

BLUE

1

2

3

4

5

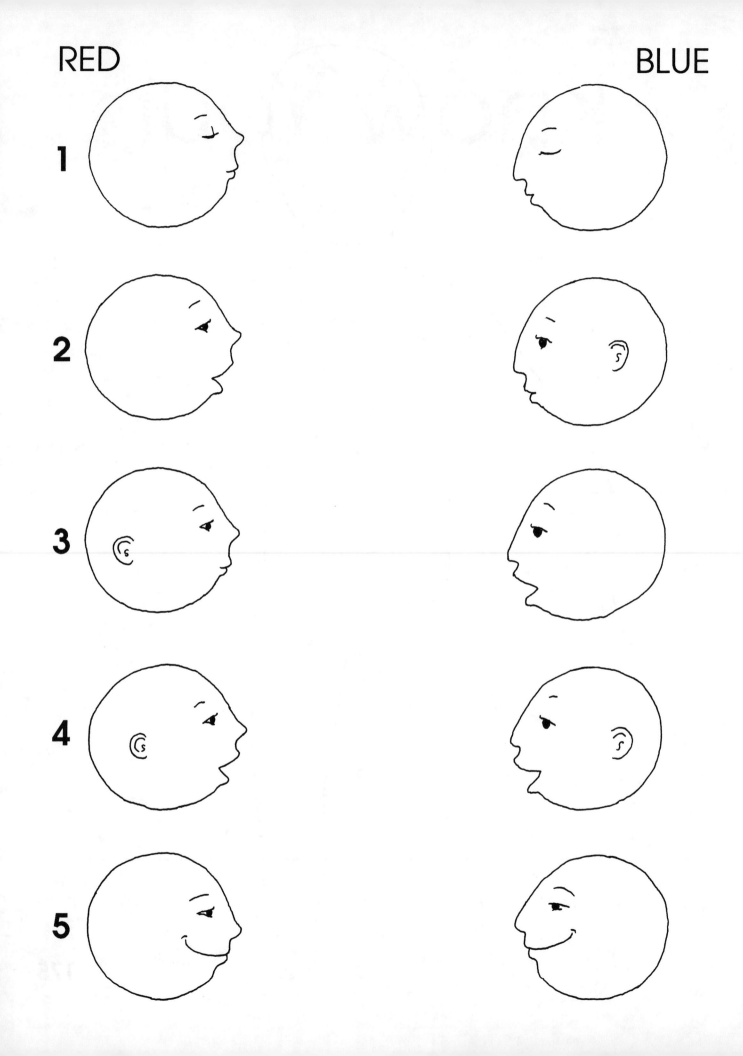

Know Your Problem

Brainstorm

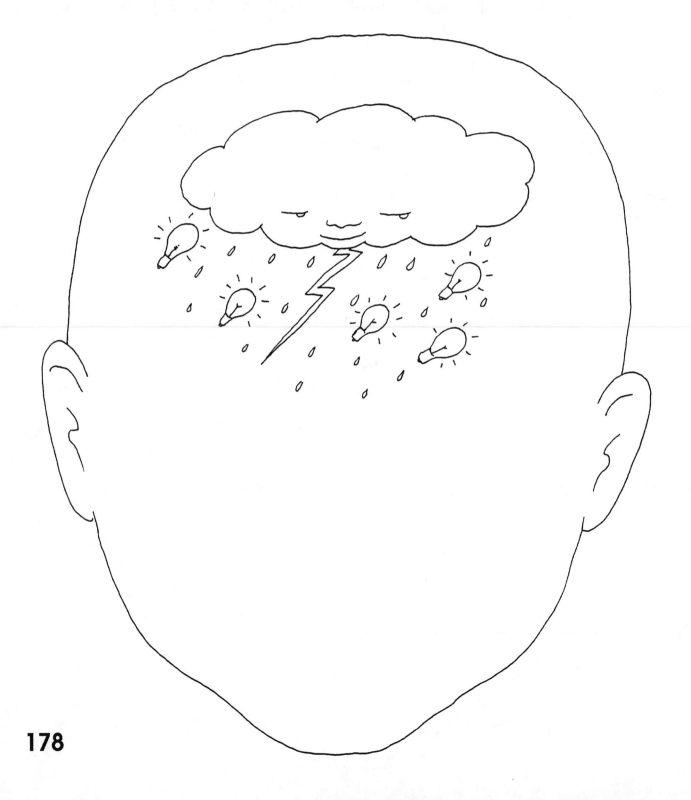

Choose

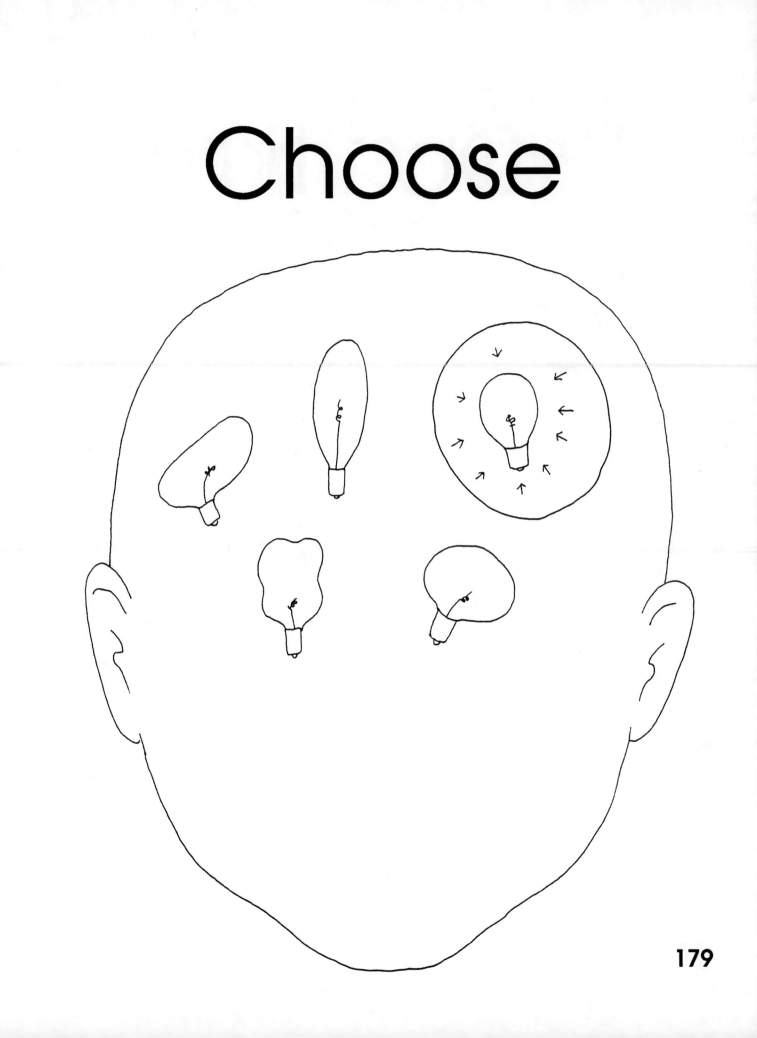

Do it!

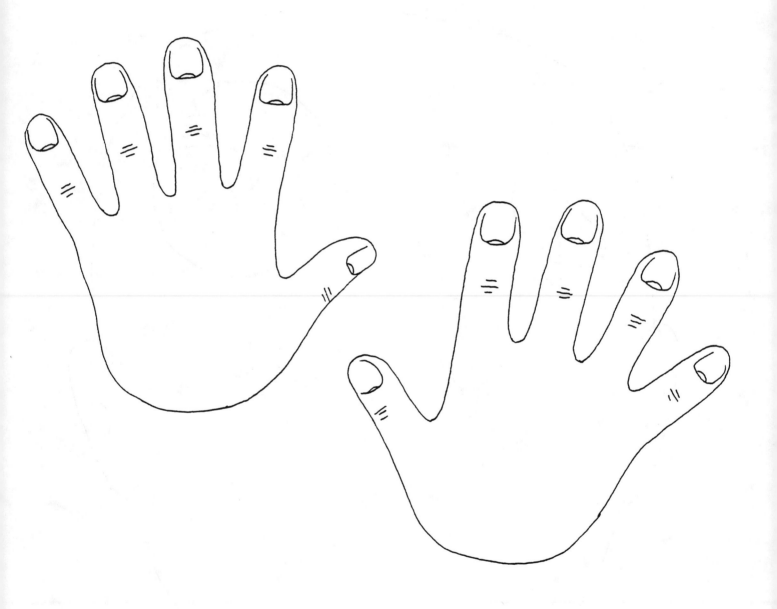

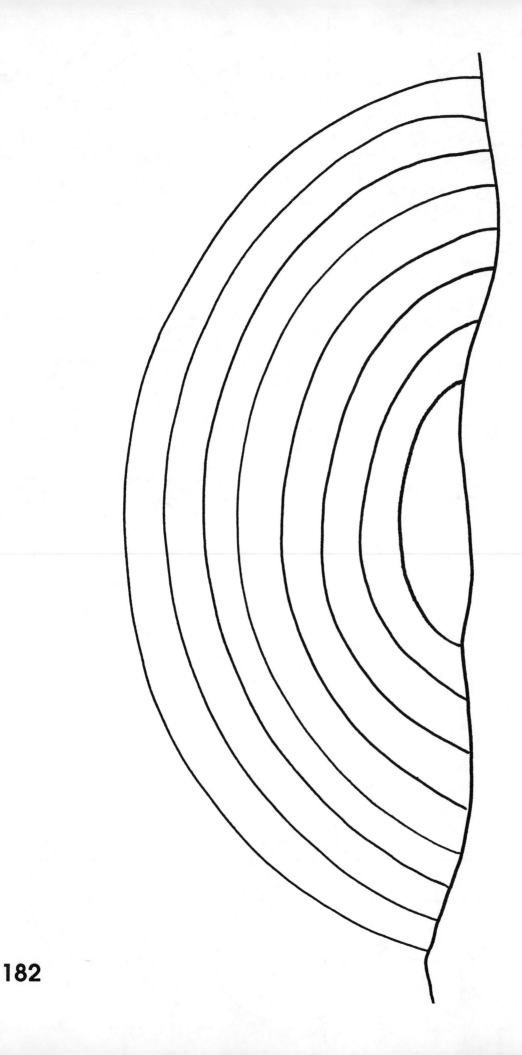

182

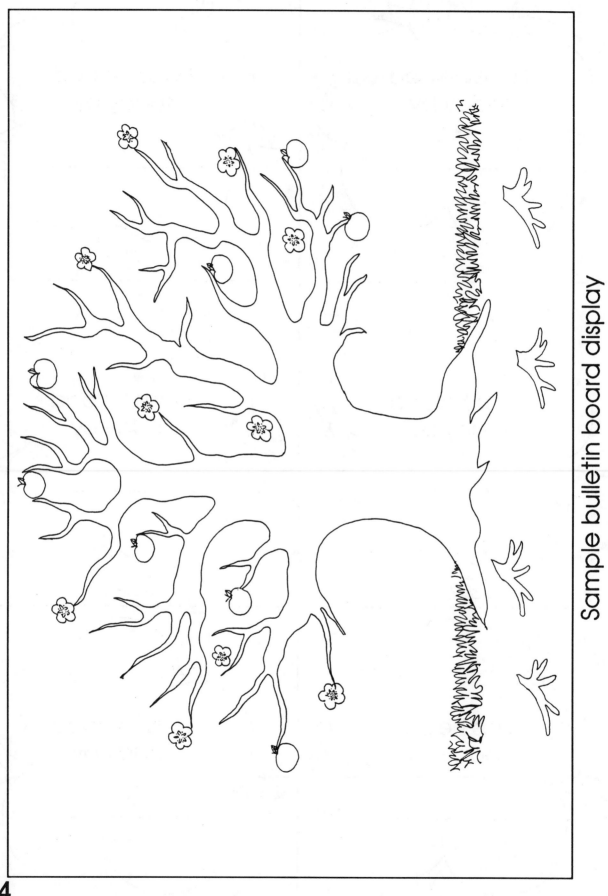

Sample bulletin board display

185

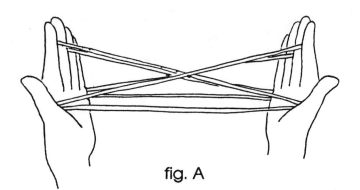

fig. A

TWO STRING FIGURES FROM CAT'S CRADLE

The game of cat's cradle probably had its origin in Asia and then spread to Europe. It is known and played in many countries around the world.

Two people and one loop of six-foot string are required. Player A takes the string and makes a loop across the palm and around the back of each hand. Player A then uses the middle fingers of each hand to pick up the string on the opposite palm (fig. A). This figure forms the *cradle.*

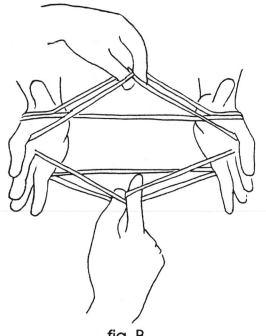

fig. B

Player B takes thumbs and index fingers and picks up the two "X"s made by the top middle sections of the cradle (looking down from above). Then Player B separates the hands and brings them outside, around, under, and up through the two bottom strings of the cradle (fig. B).

Player A gently removes his or her hands and the remaining figure is the *soldier's bed* (fig. C).

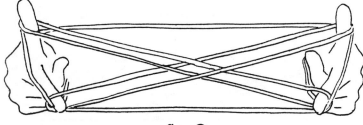

fig. C

There are six more figures in the cat's cradle sequence. Most string figures are much more complex. For detailed directions for completing the rest of cat's cradle and over 100 other figures from around the world, see *String Figures and How to Make Them* by Caroline Furness Jayne (New York: Dover Publications, 1962).

police	telephone lineworker
nurse	letter carrier
doctor	garbage collector
car mechanic	baker
dentist	firefighter
grocery store worker	teacher
gas station attendant	delivery person
counselor	sales person
farmer	musician
athlete	taxi driver
banker	janitor

Name_____

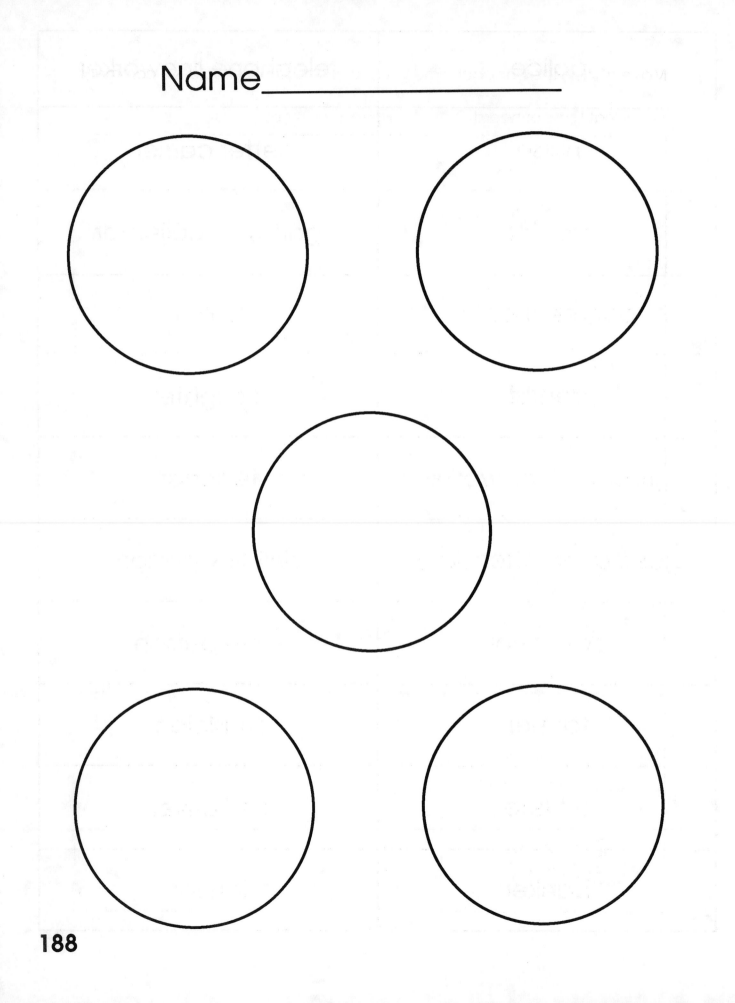

Make a "✓" in the box each time you see or hear an appreciative comment.

What I saw or heard.	How many times.
"Thank You"	
"I appreciate . . ."	
Saying thank you with a smile, hug, or handshake.	
Teachers sometimes say thank you with a note good job! or a sticker GREAT WORK!.	

A Special Gift
for you

I will _____

_____

_____

_____

Love,

Dear _____ ,
Here is a picture of
what I will do for you
as a special gift.

Love,

The greatest gift I can give you is myself, so here is my helping hand. Ask me when you want me to help you.
Love,

The greatest gift I can give you is myself, so here is my helping hand. Ask me when you want me to help you.
Love,

The greatest gift I can give you is myself, so here is my helping hand. Ask me when you want me to help you.
Love,

The greatest gift I can give you is myself, so here is my helping hand. Ask me when you want me to help you.
Love,

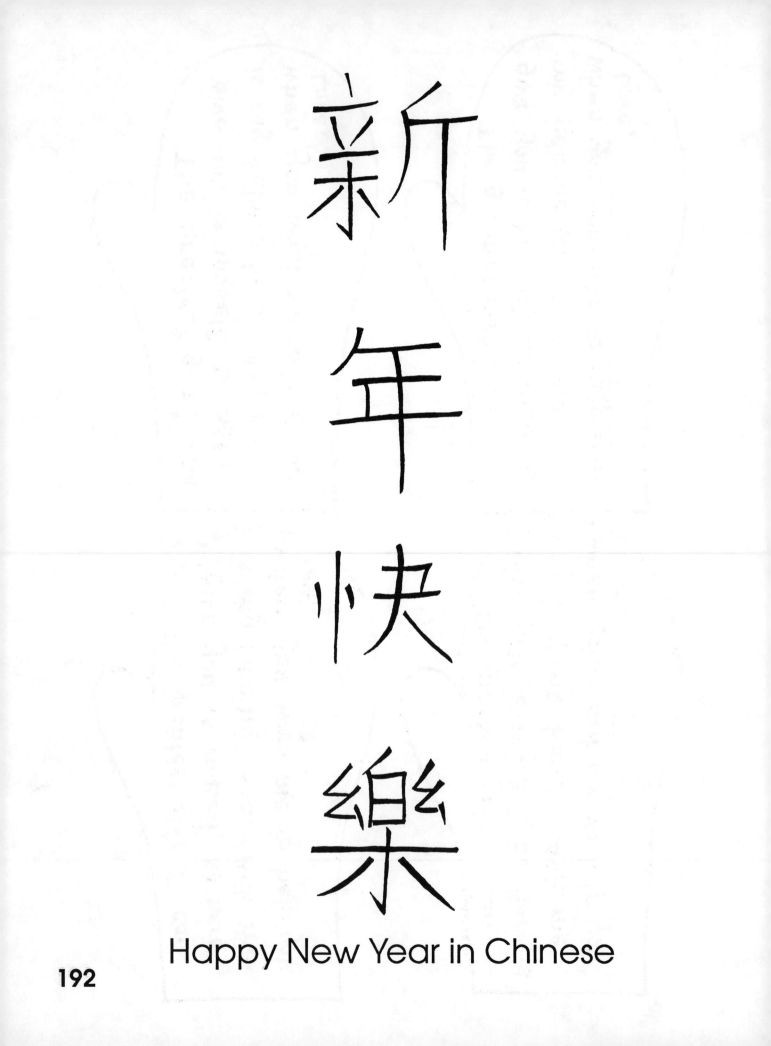

新年快樂

Happy New Year in Chinese

Dear:

We would like to invite you to bring your lunch to Room _____ on _____ at _____. This meal will be part of our studies on the Chinese New Year. Traditionally, the last meal of the old year is called the Join Together or Reunion Dinner. At this meal, the extended family shares food and games. They are also sure to leave some lucky leftovers for New Year's Day.

If you would like to join us for this celebration, please return the slip below to school with your child by _____. You may bring lunch with you or purchase it in the school cafeteria. Please also bring a small leftover of fruit or nuts to leave with the children.

We hope to see you soon!

Sincerely,

- -

Name(s)_____

I/We   will   will not   (circle one)

be attending the Chinese New Year luncheon.

Which one would you most like to give?
Which one would you most like to receive?

194

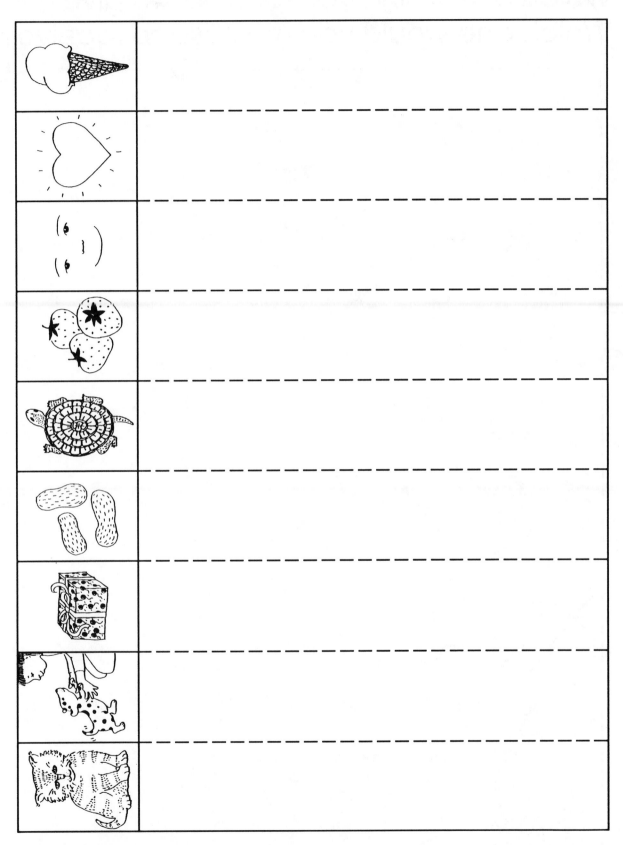

This is a sample chart. Use one sheet of cut out squares (p.194) to make a
large chart on which children can paste their chosen pictures.

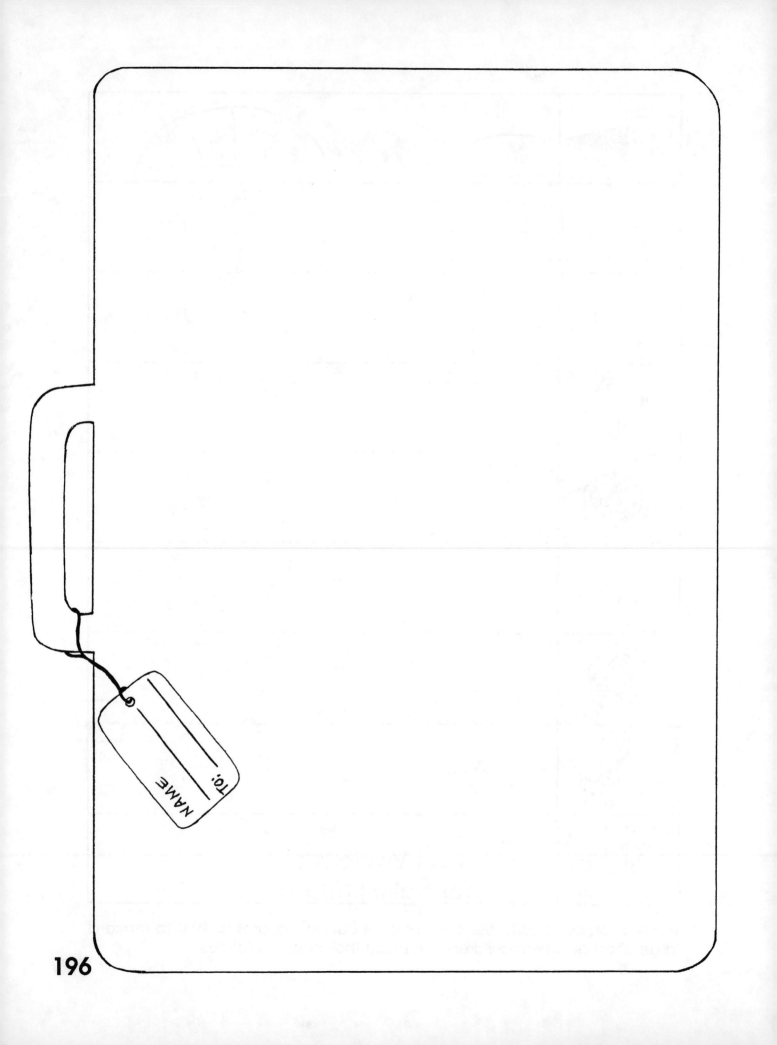

196

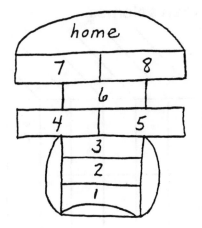

Aeroplane Hoppy

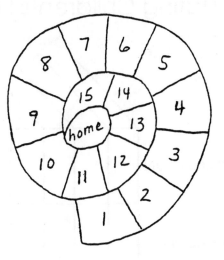

Snail Hoppy

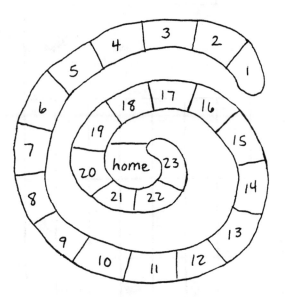

Snake Hoppy

Circle Hoppy

Rest

**Four Versions of
Australian Hoppy**

Evaluating Children's Friendship Skills and Qualities

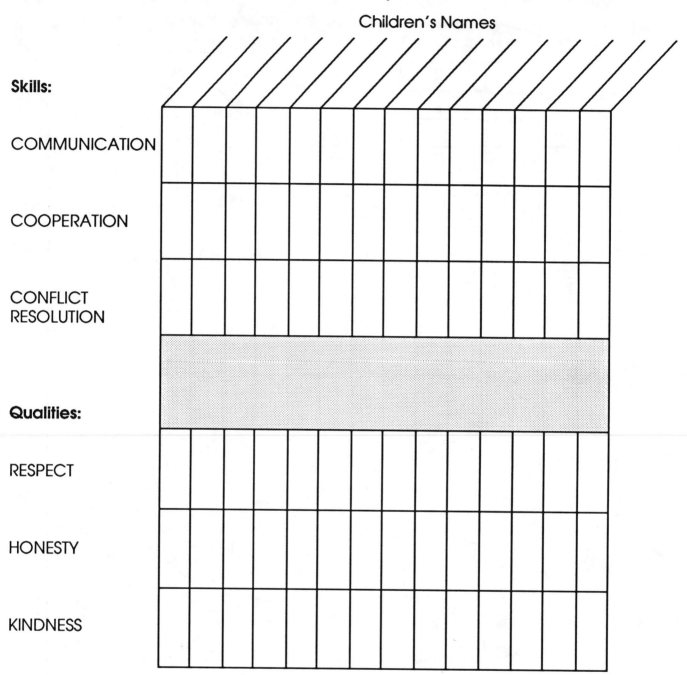

Children's Names

Skills:

COMMUNICATION

COOPERATION

CONFLICT
RESOLUTION

Qualities:

RESPECT

HONESTY

KINDNESS

Evaluating Children's Friendship Skills and Qualities

Children's Names

Skills:

Listens well

Uses I messages

Shares ideas
and objects

Encourages others

Makes decisions

Thinks critically

Thinks creatively

Solves problems

Resolves conflicts

Qualities:

Has respect for
self and others

Is honest

Is responsible

Is patient

Is kind

RESOURCES for SHARING IN THE FRIENDLY CLASSROOM

Books, games, magazines, and other materials to use with each chapter and for further reference.

Ashton-Warner, Sylvia. *Teacher.* New York: Simon & Schuster, 1963.

Briggs, Dorothy Corkville. *Your Child's Self-Esteem.* New York: Doubleday, 1970.

Brown, George Isaac. *Human Teaching for Human Learning.* New York: Penguin Books, 1978.

Canfield, J., and H. Wells. *100 Ways to Enhance Self Concept in the Classroom.* Englewood Cliffs, N.J.: Prentice-Hall, 1976.

Canfield, J., with Ellen Fleischmann et al. *Self Esteem in the Classroom.* Pacific Palisades, Calif.: Self-Esteem Seminars, 1986.

Crary, Richard E. *Humanizing the School: Curriculum Development and Theory.* New York: Alfred A. Knopf, Inc., 1969.

Deranja, Michael Nitai. *The Art of Joyful Education.* Nevada City, Calif.: Ananda How-to-Live Schools, 1980.

Ginott, Haim. *Teacher and Child.* New York: Macmillan and Co., 1972.

Glasser, William. *Schools Without Failure.* New York: Harper and Row, 1969.

Goodlad, John. *A Place Called School: Prospects for the Future.* New York: McGraw-Hill, 1984.

Gordon, Thomas. *Teacher Effectiveness Training.* New York: Peter Wyden, 1974.

Greer, Mary, and Bonnie Rubenstein. *Will the Real Teacher Please Stand Up.* Pacific Palisades, Calif.: Goodyear Publishing Company, 1972.

Harmin, Merrill, and Sax Saville. *A Peaceable Classroom.* Minneapolis: Winston Press, 1977.

Hendricks, Gay, and James Fadiman. *Transpersonal Education.* Englewood Cliffs, N.J.: Prentice-Hall, 1975.

Jackson, Philip. *Life in Classrooms.* New York: Holt, Rinehart, and Winston, 1968.

Kohl, Herbert. *Growing Minds: On Becoming a Teacher.* New York: Harper and Row, 1984.

Moustakas, Clark. *The Authentic Teacher.* Cambridge, Mass.: Howard A. Doyle Publishing Co., 1972.

Parsons, Cynthia. *Seeds: Some Good Ways to Improve Schools.* Santa Barbara, Calif.: Woodbridge Press, 1985.

Postman, Neil, and Charles Weingartner. *Teaching as a Subversive Activity.* New York: Delacorte Press, 1969.

Romey, William D. *Risk-Trust-Love: Learning in a Humane Environment.* Columbus, Ohio: Charles E. Merrill, 1972.

Toffler, Alvin. *The Third Wave.* New York: William Morrow, 1980.

Weinstein, Gerald, and Mario Fantini. *Toward Humanistic Education: A Curriculum of Affect.* New York: Praeger Publishers, 1970.

RESOURCES for FRIENDSHIP FOR YOUNG CHILDREN

Damon, William. *The Social World of the Child.* San Francisco: Jossey-Bass, 1977.

___. *Social and Personality Development.* New York: W. W. Norton, 1983.

Edwards, Carolyn Pope. *Promoting Social and Moral Development in Young Children.* New York: Teachers College Press, 1986.

Eisenberg, Nancy, and Paul H. Mussen. *The Roots of Prosocial Behavior in Children.* Cambridge, Mass.: Harvard University Press, 1989.

Galbraith, Ronald E., and Thomas M. Jones. *Moral Reasoning: A Teaching Handbook for Adapting Kohlberg to the Classroom.* Anoka, Minn.: Greenhaven Press, 1976.

Kohlberg, Lawrence. *Child Psychology and Childhood Education.* New York: Longman, 1987.

Lickona, Thomas, ed. *Moral Development and Behavior.* New York: Holt, Rinehart, and Winston, 1976.

___. *Raising Good Children.* New York: Bantam, 1983.

Mussen, Paul, and Nancy Eisenberg-Berg. *Roots of Caring, Sharing, and Helping.* San Francisco: W.H. Freeman, 1977.

Piaget, Jean. *The Moral Judgment of the Child.* New York: The Free Press, 1965.

Rubin, Zick. *Children's Friendships.* Cambridge, Mass.: Harvard University Press, 1980.

Selman, Robert. *The Growth of Interpersonal Understanding.* New York: Academic Press, 1980.

RESOURCES for COMMUNICATION, COOPERATION, AND CONFLICT RESOLUTION

Abrams, Grace, and Fran Schmidt. *Peace Is in Our Hands.* The Jane Addams Peace Association, 1213 Race Street, Philadelphia, Pennsylvania 19107 (1974).

Animal Town Game Company, P.O. Box 2002, Santa Barbara, California 93120. Cooperative Game Company.

Carpenter, Susan. *A Repertoire of Peacemaking Skills.* Boulder: University of Colorado, COPRED, 1977.

Carlsson-Paige, Nancy, and Diane Levin. *The War Play Dilemma.* New York: Teachers College Press, 1987.

___. *Who's Calling the Shots? How to Respond Effectively to Children's Fascination with War Play and War Toys.* Philadelphia: New Society Publishers, 1989.

Chase, Larry. *The Other Side of the Report Card: A How To Do It Program for Affective Education.* Glenville, Ill.: Scott, Foresman, 1975.

Chihak, Mary, and Barbara Jackson Heron. *Games Children Should Play: Sequential Lessons for Teaching Communication Skills.* Santa Monica, Calif.: Goodyear, 1980.

Cohen, Elizabeth. *Designing Groupwork: Strategies for the Heterogeneous Classroom.* New York: Teachers College Press, 1986.

Cortes, Carlos. *Global Perspectives: Education for a World in Change.* New York: The American Forum, 1980.

Curle, Adam. *Making Peace.* London: Tavistock, 1971.

Dreikurs, Rudolph. *Children: The Challenge.* New York: Duell, Sloan, and Pearce, 1964.

___. *Logical Consequences: A Handbook of Discipline.* New York: Harper and Row, 1971.

___. *Maintaining Sanity in the Classroom.* New York: Harper and Row, 1971.

Drew, Naomi. *Learning the Skills of Peacemaking: An Activity Guide for Elementary Age Children.* Rolling Hills Estates, Calif.: Jalmar Press, 1987.

Educators for Social Responsibility. *Perspectives: A Teaching Guide to Concepts of Peace.* Cambridge, Mass.: ESR, 1983.

___. *Taking Part.* Cambridge, Mass.: ESR, 1984.

Fagen, Stanley A., et al. *Teaching Children Self-Control.* Columbus, Ohio: Charles Merrill, 1975.

Family Pastimes, R.R. 4, Perth, Ontario, Canada, K7H 3C6. Cooperative Game Company.

Filley, Alan C. *Interpersonal Conflict Resolution.* Glenview, Ill.: Scott Foresman, 1975.

Fisher, Roger. *International Conflict for Beginners.* New York: Harper and Row, 1969.

Fisher, Roger, and William Ury. *Getting to Yes: Negotiating Agreements Without Giving In.* Boston: Houghton Mifflin, 1981.

Flugelman, Andrew. *The New Games Book.* New York: Doubleday, 1976.

Hurt, Thomas, et al. *Communication in the Classroom.* Reading, Mass.: Addison Wesley, 1978.

Johnson, David, and Roger Johnson. *Circles of Learning: Cooperation in the Classroom.* Alexandria, Va.: Association for Supervision and Curriculum Development, 1984.

___. *Learning Together and Alone: Cooperation, Competition, and Individualization.* Englewood Cliffs, N.J.: Prentice-Hall, 1975.

Judson, Stephanie, ed. *A Manual on Non-Violence and Children.* Non-Violence and Children Program, 1515 Cherry St., Philadelphia, Pennsylvania 19102 (1977).

Kreidler, William J. *Creative Conflict Resolution: Over 200 Activities for a More Peaceful Classroom.* Glenview, Ill.: Scott Foresman, 1983.

McGinnis, James, and Kathleen McGinnis. *Educating for Peace and Justice: A Handbook for Teachers.* St. Louis: Institute for Peace and Justice, 1981.

Moorman, Chick, and Dee Dishon. *Our Classroom: We Can Learn Together.* Englewood Cliffs, N.J.: Prentice-Hall, 1983.

Orlick, Terry. *The Cooperative Sports and Games Book.* New York: Pantheon Books, 1978.

___. *The Second Cooperative Sports and Games Book.* New York: Pantheon Books, 1982.

Prutzman, P., et al. *The Friendly Classroom for a Small Planet.* Philadelphia: New Society Publishers, 1988.

Reardon, Betty, ed. *Educating for Global Responsibility: Teacher-Designed Curricula for Peace Education K-12.* New York: Teachers College Press, 1988.

Schmidt, Fran. *Creative Conflict Solving for Kids.* Grace Contrino Abrams Peace Education Foundation, Inc., Box 19-1153, Miami Beach, Florida 33119 (1982).

Schniedewind, Nancy, and Ellen Davidson. *Cooperative Learning, Cooperative Lives: A Sourcebook of Learning Activities for Building a Peaceful World.* Dubuque, Iowa: Wm. C. Brown Co., 1987.

Schuncke, George M., and Suzanne Lowell Krogh. *Helping Children Choose: Resources, Strategies, and Activities for Teachers of Young Children.* Glenview, Ill.: Scott Foresman, 1983.

Shutter, Robert. *Understanding Misunderstandings: Exploring Interpersonal Communication.* New York: Harper and Row, 1979.

Stanford, Barbara, ed. *Peacemaking.* New York: Bantam Books, 1976.

Stanford, Gene. *Developing Effective Classroom Groups.* New York: Hart Publishers, 1977.

Stanford, G., and A. Roark. *Human Interaction in Education.* Boston: Allyn and Bacon, Inc., 1974.

Wilt, Joy, and Bill Watson. *Relationship Builders.* Waco, Texas: Word, 1978.

RESOURCES for FRIENDSHIP IN THE CURRICULUM

Rainbows

For Teachers

Graham, F. Lanier. *The Rainbow Book.* New York: Random House, 1975.

Greeler, Robert. *Rainbows, Halos, and Glories.* Boston: Cambridge University Press, 1980.

Heuer, Kenneth. *Rainbows, Halos, and Other Wonders.* New York: Dodd, 1978.

For Children

De Rico, Ul. *Rainbow Goblins.* New York: Warner, 1979.

Freeman, Don. *A Rainbow of My Own.* New York: Viking, 1966.

Gilder, Jean. *Tom and the Magic Rainbow.* London: Medici Society, Ltd., 1981.

Hillert, Margaret. *Run to the Rainbow.* Cleveland: Modern Curriculum Press, 1980.

Kwitz, Mary DeBall. *When It Rains.* New York: Follett, 1974.

Marino, Dorothy Bronson. *Buzzy Bear and the Rainbow.* New York: Watts, 1962.

McCoy, James C. *Darby's Rainbow.* Los Altos Hills, Calif.: Davenport, 1988.

Zolotow, Charlotte. *The Storm Book.* New York: Harper, 1952.

Plants

Challand, Helen. *Plants Without Seeds.* San Francisco: Children's Press, 1986.

Gale, Frank C., and Clarice Gale. *Experiences with Plants for Young Children.* Palo Alto, Calif.: Pacific Books, 1975.

Harding, Diana. *Some Plants Have Funny Names.* New York: Crown 1983.

Miner, Irene. *Plants We Know.* San Francisco: Children's Press, 1981.

Nussbaum, Hedda. *Plants Do Amazing Things.* New York: Random House, 1977.

Selsam, Millicent E. *Eat the Fruit, Plant the Seed.* New York: William Morrow, 1980.

Webster, Vera. *Plant Experiments.* San Francisco: Children's Press, 1982.

Alphabet Books

Anno, Mitsumasa. *Anno's Alphabet: An Adventure in Imagination.* New York: Harper and Row, 1975.

Boynton, Sandra. *A Is for Angry.* New York: Workman, 1983.

Burningham, John. *John Burningham's ABC.* New York: Crown, 1986.

Decker, Dorothy. *Stripe Presents the ABC's.* Minneapolis: Dillon Press, 1984.

Duke, Kate. *Guinea Pig ABC.* New York: Dutton, 1983.

Hoban, Tana. *A, B, See!* New York: Greenwillow, 1982.

Milgrom, Harry. *ABC of Ecology.* New York: Macmillan, 1972.

Sendak, Maurice. *Alligators All Around.* New York: Harper and Row, 1962.

Van Allsburg, Chris. *The Z Was Zapped.* Boston: Houghton Mifflin, 1987.

Wildsmith, Brian. *ABC.* New York: Watts, 1962.

Community Helpers

Alten, Jerry. *Community Friends.* Carthage, Ill.: Good Apple, 1983.

Berridge, Celia. *On My Street.* New York: Random House, 1987.

Cherryholmes, C., and G. Manson. *Our Communities.* New York: McGraw-Hill, 1979.

Clapsdale, Mark, and Gail Aemmer. *Community Helpers Fun Book.* Greensborough, N.C.: Carson-Dellos, 1984.

Gibbons, Gail. *Fill It Up! All About Service Stations.* New York: Crowell, 1985. Also by Gail Gibbons: *Fire Fire* (Crowell, 1984), *Farming* (New York: Holiday House, 1988), *The Post Office Book* (New York: Harper and Row, 1986), *Department Store* (Crowell, 1984), and *Trucks* (Crowell, 1981).

Kalman, Bobby. *I Live in a City.* New York: Crabtree Publishing, 1986.

RESOURCES for FRIENDLY HOLIDAYS

Beckman, Carol, Roberta Simmons, and Nancy Thomas. *Channels to Children: An Early Childhood Activity Guide for Holidays and Seasons.* Colorado Springs: Channels to Children, 1982.

Bragdon, Allen D., and UNICEF. *Joy Through the World.* New York: Dodd, Mead, and Co., 1985.

Cohen, Hennig, and Tristan Potter Coffin, eds. *The Folklore of American Holidays.* Detroit: Gale Research Co., 1987.

Manning-Sanders, Ruth. *Festivals.* New York: E.P. Dutton, 1973.

Shannon-Thornberry, Milo. *The Alternate Celebrations Catalogue.* New York: The Pilgrim Press, 1982.

Van Straalen, Alice. *The Book of Holidays Around the World.* New York: E.P. Dutton, 1986.

RESOURCES for A WORLD OF FRIENDS and OUR HUMAN FAMILY

Abruscato, Joe, and Jack Hassard. *The Earth People Activity Book.* Santa Monica, Calif.: Goodyear, 1978.

Back, Don, et al. *Global Horizons: A Global Education Resource Directory.* Amherst, Mass.: University of Massachusetts, Center for International Education, 1988.

Baker, Gwendolyn Calvert. *Planning and Organizing for Multi-cultural Instruction.* Reading, Mass.: Addison-Wesley, 1983.

Banks, James A. *Teaching Strategies for Ethnic Studies.* Boston: Allyn and Bacon, 1975.

Caballero, Jane, and Derek Whordley. *Children Around the World.* Humanics Limited, Box 74, Atlanta, Georgia 30309.

Cole, Ann, et al. *Children Are Children Are Children.* Boston: Little Brown and Co., 1978.

Cooney, Barbara. *Miss Rumphius.* New York: Puffin Books, 1985.

Davidson, Ellen, and Nancy Schniedewind. *Open Minds to Equality: Learning Activities to Promote Race, Sex, Class, and Age Equity.* Englewood Cliffs, N.J.: Prentice-Hall, 1983.

Derman-Sparks, Louise, and the A.B.C. Task Force. *Anti-Bias Curriculum: Tools for Empowering Young Children.* Washington, D.C.: National Association for the Education of Young Children, 1989.

FACES: The Magazine about People. Cobblestone Publishing Inc., 20 Grove St., Peterborough, New Hampshire 03458.

Fiarotta, Phyllis, and Noel Fiarotta. *The You and Me Heritage Tree: Ethnic Crafts for Children.* New York: Workman, 1976.

Gibbons, Maurice, and Sharlene Lazin. *The Universal Curriculum Teaching Action and Idea Book.* Burnaby, B.C., Canada: Simon Fraser University, World Citizens for a Universal Curriculum, 1986.

Haskins, Jim. *Count Your Way Through Japan.* Minneapolis, Minn.: Carolrhoda Books, 1987.

How People Live Series. Lexington, Mass.: Schoolhouse Press, 1986.

Lee, Nancy, and Linda Oldham. *Hands On Heritage.* Hands On Publications, 7061 Mariner Way, Long Beach, California.

Massachusetts Global Education Project. *Global Issues in the Elementary Classroom.* Denver: Center for Teaching International Relations, 1988.

McNeill, Earldene, Velma Schmidt, and Judy Allen. *Cultural Awareness for Young Children.* Dallas, Texas: Learning Tree, 1975.

Rainbow Activities: 50 Multicultural/ Human Relations Experiences. South El Monte, Calif.: Creative Teaching Press, 1977.

Skipping Stones Magazine. 80574 Hazleton Road, Cottage Grove, Oregon 97424.

Spier, Peter. *People.* New York: Doubleday, 1980.

UNICEF. Information Center on Children's Cultures, 331 East 38th Street, New York 10016.

UNICEF has a wealth of materials available for human family studies. The following information sheets have suitable activities and resources for the primary classroom. Some of the activities in the units for grades 4-6 can be adapted. These are all available for a small fee from the address above.

Pen Pals and Other Exchanges

Head to Toes—An International Unit on Adornment, Grades K-3

Children At Work—A Mini-unit for Grades 4-6

Let's Play—An International Unit on Games for Grades 4-6

An International Program on Clothing, K-3

A Development Unit for Grades K-3

A Bibliography of Materials Useful for Teaching an International Unit in Grades K-3 on Family

Pictorial Materials: Children Around the World

Songs and Dances Around the World

Shelter

Sources of Children's Books from Other Countries and in Other Languages

An International Unit for Grades 4-6—Feasts, Festivals and Celebrations

The New Year Around the World—Program for Grades 4-6

Religious and Social Meaning of Names—A Mini-unit for Ages 5-8.

*Making Music Around the World—An International Unit
 for Grades K-3*

UNICEF also sells slides, pictures, puzzles, games, coloring books, and other teaching materials. Write for a catalog.

RESOURCES for FRIENDSHIP QUILT PROJECT

Children's Books

Bayley, Nicola, and William Mayne. *The Patchwork Cat.* New York: Knopf, 1981.

Berenstain, Stan, and Jan Berenstain. *The Berenstain Bears and Mama's New Job.* New York: Random House, 1984.

Chorao, Kate. *Kate's Quilt.* New York: Dutton, 1982.

Ernst, Lisa Campbell. *Sam Johnson and the Blue Ribbon Quilt.* New York: Lothrop, Lee, and Shepard Books, 1983.

Fair, Sylvia. *The Bedspread.* New York: William Morrow, 1982.

Flournoy, Valerie. *The Patchwork Quilt.* New York: Dutton, 1985.

Johnston, Tony, and Tomie dePaola. *The Quilt Story.* New York: Putnam, 1985.

Jonas, Ann. *The Quilt.* New York: Greenwillow, 1984.

Roth, Susan, and Ruth Phang. *Patchwork Tales.* New York: Atheneum, 1984.

RESOURCES for CHILD'S PLAY

Avedon, E. M., and Brian Sutton-Smith, eds. *The Study of Games.* New York: Wiley and Sons, 1971.

Herron, R. E., and Brian Sutton-Smith, eds. *Child's Play.* New York: Wiley and Sons, 1971.

Jayne, Caroline Furness. *String Figures and How to Make Them.* New York: Dover Publications, 1962.

Lancy, David F., and Allan B. Tindall. *The Anthropological Study of Play: Problems and Prospects.* Cornwall, N.Y.: Leisure Press, 1976.

Scwartzman, Helen. *Transformations: The Anthropology of Children's Play.* New York: Plenum Press, 1978.

Sutton-Smith, Brian. *The Folkgames of Children.* Austin: University of Texas, 1972.

FILMS ON PLAY AND GAMES IN MANY CULTURES
are available for rent from:

Audio Visual Services, 17 Willard Building, Pennsylvania State University, University Park, Pennsylvania 16802.

University of California, Extension Media Center, Berkeley, California 94720.

Documentary Educational Resources, Inc., 101 Morse Street, Watertown, Massachusetts 02143.

BOOKS ON FRIENDSHIP FOR YOUNG CHILDREN

Hundreds of books for young children incorporate the theme of friendship. The following books are those that I have come to know and enjoy. Many of them focus on specific problems children encounter in relating such as having a friend move, feeling lonely or isolated, and the difficulties in threesomes. I have also included books that focus on conflict resolution and peacemaking. I am continually searching for books that explore multicultural and interracial friendship, a number of which are annotated in this section.

Some of these books are classics; others may no longer be in print. Your school and community library should have many of these titles. If you want a special book, most books can be ordered through a local interlibrary loan service.

I plan to update this resource list periodically and welcome information on books that you enjoy using with the young children in your classroom. Please send the book title, author, publisher, copyright date, and brief annotation to me in c/o

> Joining Hands Book List
> 140 Armory Street
> Keene, New Hampshire 03431

Anglund, Joan Walsh. *Love Is a Special Way of Feeling.* New York: Harcourt Brace Jovanovich, 1960. This is a delightful little book describing many ways to feel love.

Alexander, Martha. *I Sure Am Glad to See You Blackboard Bear.* New York: Dial, 1976. An imaginary bear helps a little boy solve problems with his playmates.

Aliki. *We Are Best Friends.* New York: Greenwillow Books, 1982. Robert says to Peter, "You can't move away. We're best friends." But Peter does and both boys make new friends in time.

___. *Feelings.* New York: Mulberry Books, 1987. Through amusing cartoons and true-to-life vignettes, Aliki shares with us the child's world of feelings.

Ardizzone, Edward. *Lucy Brown and Mr. Grimes.* New York: H. Z. Walck, 1971. An orphan girl and old Mr. Grimes are both lonely until one day they meet in the park and become friends.

Battles, Edith. *One to Teeter-Totter.* Chicago: Whitman, 1973. A little boy discovers that the best thing about his teeter-totter is a friend to share it with.

___. *What Does the Rooster Say, Yoshio?* Chicago: Whitman, 1978. A Japanese boy and an American girl have trouble communicating.

Brandenberg, Franz. *Nice New Neighbors.* New York: Greenwillow, 1977. The fieldmouse children, at first rejected, use persistence and creativity and are finally accepted by their new neighbors.

Brown, Marc. *Moose and Goose.* New York: Dutton, 1978. Moose lives upstairs and likes to tap dance. Goose lives downstairs and likes to sleep. Their noisy dilemma is creatively resolved.

Bunting, Eve. *Clancy's Coat.* New York: Frederick Warne, 1984. Tippet and Clancy are two old friends who finally have their first quarrel and then gradually mend their friendship.

Charlip, Remy, and Burton Supree. *Harlequin and the Gift of Many Colors.* New York: Parents Magazine Press, 1973. Harlequin can not go to the carnival because he is too poor to have a costume. His friends give Harlequin pieces of their costumes and when they are sewn together he becomes a rainbow of colors, clothed "in the love of his friends."

Child Study Children's Book Committee at Bank Street, eds. *Friends Are Like That! - Stories to Read to Yourself.* New York: Crowell, 1979. This is a fine collection of nine stories and a poem by such noted authors as Astrid Lindgren, John Steptoe, and Charlotte Zolotow.

Clifton, Lucille. *My Friend Jacob.* New York: Dutton, 1980. A young boy tells about Jacob, who, though older and mentally slower, helps him a lot and is his very best friend.

Cohen, Miriam. *It's George.* New York: Greenwillow, 1988. George, a first grader, is not accepted by all his classmates until he develops local fame by saving the life of his elderly friend. The other titles in this series on a multiethnic first grade class all deal with relationships. See especially *Will I Have a Friend?*, *Best Friends*, and *Jim's Dog Muffins.*

Cooney, Barbara. *Miss Rumphius.* New York: Puffin Books, 1988. This award-winning story follows Miss Rumphius around the world and then back to her home by the sea where she finds a way to make the world more beautiful.

cummings, e.e. *Fairy Tales.* New York: Harcourt Brace Jovanovich, 1965. Here are four delightful original tales that tell of special relationships between an elephant and a butterfly, a bird and an empty house, and two little girls named I and You.

Dauer, Rosamond. *Bullfrog Builds a House.* New York: Greenwillow, 1977. Not wanting to forget any important items for his new house, Bullfrog seeks the advice of his friend Gertrude. He almost forgets the most important thing—their friendship.

Delton, Judy. *Three Friends Find Spring.* New York: Crown, 1977. Rabbit and Squirrel try to create an early spring for their friend Duck who has a bad case of the winter doldrums.

___. *Two Good Friends.* New York: Crown, 1986. Duck and Bear have their differences but learn to share their talents.

___. *Two Is Company.* New York: Crown, 1976. Bear feels that his friendship with Duck is threatened when a chipmunk moves into the neighborhood.

dePaola, Tomie. *Bill and Pete.* New York: G. P. Putnam and Sons, 1978. This is an amusing story of an unlikely friendship between a crocodile and a supportive bird who serves as his toothbrush.

___. *The Hunter and the Animals.* New York: Holiday House, 1981. This is a wordless picture book in which a hunter is befriended by the animals he was going to shoot. Seeing that they are his friends, the hunter breaks his gun.

Desbarats, Peter. *Gabrielle and Selena.* New York: Harcourt, 1968. This is the humorous story of two eight-year-old girls, one black and the other white, who show up in each other's homes in an exchange of identity for the evening.

Duvoisin, Roger Antoine. *Periwinkle.* New York: Alfred A. Knopf, 1976. A giraffe and a frog learn that friendship means listening as well as talking.

Emberley, Barbara. *Drummer Hoff.* Englewood Cliffs, N.J.: Prentice-Hall, 1967. This is a folk tale about the loading and firing of a cannon. Adults will need to help children analyze the story to come to the intended conclusion.

Ehrlich, Amy. *Leo, Zack, and Emmie.* New York: Dial Press, 1987. This is a story that explores the problems shared by three friends in a world that seems designed for pairs. See also *Leo, Zack, and Emmie Together Again.*

Eisenberg, Phyllis Rose. *A Mitzvah Is Something Special.* New York: Harper and Row, 1978. Lisa's two grandmothers are very different from one another but they both enjoy it when Lisa does a mitzvah or good deed.

Fitzhugh, Louise, and Sandra Scoppetone. *Bang, Bang, You're Dead.* New York: Harper and Row, 1969. Two groups of boys are battling over the use of a hill for a make-believe war. When some of the children get hurt they learn to make peace.

Friedman, Ina R. *How My Parents Learned to Eat.* Boston: Houghton Mifflin, 1984. A young child explains how her American sailor father and her Japanese mother developed a friendship by learning to eat in each other's ways.

Erskine, Jim. *Bert and Susie's Messy Tale.* New York: Crown 1979. Bert and Susie play in a mud puddle and almost miss the flower show.

Goffstein, M. B. *Neighbors.* New York: Harper and Row, 1979. After several false starts, two women gradually become friends.

Goldsmith, Howard. *Welcome Makato.* Northvale, N.J.: Santillana Publishing Company, 1983. Makato, a boy from Japan, moves into an international neighborhood. As he and the other children become friends they learn about cultural differences. This book is one of the Friends and Neighbors series, which all take place in the same neighborhood. Other titles are *Stormy Day Together, The Contest,* and *Little Lost Dog.*

Hazen, Barbara S. *Why Couldn't I Be an Only Kid Like You, Wigger?* New York: Atheneum, 1975. Two different views on the advantages and disadvantages of being an only child are amusingly presented.

Hays, Wilma Pitchford. *Yellow Fur and Little Hawk.* New York: Coward, 1980. The story of a devastating drought focuses on the friendship of a Native American and a white.

Heide, Florence Parry. *Sound of Sunshine, Sound of Rain.* New York: Parents Magazine Press, 1970. This is the story of a little blind black boy who finds a new friend in the park. This book teaches children that the world is just a reflection of the ways we wish to see it.

Henkes, Kevin. *Chester's Way.* New York: Greenwillow, 1988. Chester and his best friend Wilson learn to include their neighbor Lilly in friendship and play.

Hickman, Martha Whitmore. *My Friend William Moved Away.* New York: Abingdon, 1979. Jimmy misses his friend William when he moves.

Hirsh, Marilyn. *Captain Jiri and Rabbi Jacob.* New York: Holiday, 1976. Two different men find they can work together and profit from each other's company.

Hoban, Russell. *The Brute Family.* New York: Macmillan, 1976. Baby Brute brings home *a good feeling* that changes the grouchy Brute family.

Hoffman, Phyllis. *Steffie and Me.* New York: Harper and Row, 1970. Two children, one black and the other white, enjoy everyday activities together.

Holabird, Katherine. *Angelina and Alice.* New York: Potter, 1987. Two mice friends work out their differences and discover the importance of teamwork in an acrobatics show.

Hurwitz, Johanna. *Busybody Nora.* New York: Morrow, 1976. Six-year-old Nora lives in an apartment building in New York City. She wants to get to know all her neighbors, most of whom are friendly, except for one woman who calls her a busybody.

___. *New Neighbors for Nora.* New York: Morrow, 1979. Nora, hoping to make a new friend, is not too happy when Eugene Spencer Eastman moves into her building.

Hutchins, Pat. *Changes, Changes.* New York: Collier, 1971. This wordless picture book tells the story of a toy wooden couple building their own house. When it burns down, they cooperate to build it again.

Ichikawa, Satomi. *Friends.* New York: Parents Magazine Press, 1976. "We need friends for jumping over and bumping over." So begins this delightful exploration of how friends stick together through thick or thin.

Jaynes, Ruth. *Friends! Friends! Friends!* Glendale, Calif.: Bowmar, 1967. We follow an oriental kindergarten girl through her school day, meeting her friends of various ages and races. Real photographs enhance the story.

Kalman, Bobbie. *Fun with My Friends.* New York: Crabtree Publishing, 1985. This book on multicultural friendship includes questions to discuss and an activity at the end. Other titles by Kalman from the In My World Series are *People in My Family, Happy to Be Me, Our Earth, People and Places,* and *I Live in a City.*

Keats, Ezra Jack. *Apt. 3.* New York: Macmillan, 1971. Two brothers, investigating the various sounds of an apartment building, find a friend in Mr. Muntz, the blind man behind the door of Apt. 3.

___. *A Letter to Amy.* New York: Harper, 1968. A boy faces a dilemma when he wants to invite a girl to his all-boy birthday party.

___. *Maggie and the Pirate.* New York: Four Winds Press, 1979. Maggie comes to understand why the Pirate, a new kid, steals her pet cricket.

Kingman, Lee. *Peter's Long Walk.* New York: Doubleday, 1953. Peter searches for new friends. The story is told in repetitive text and charming pictures.

Krahn, Fernando. *The Great Ape.* New York: Viking Press, 1978. A little girl develops a friendship with an enormous ape on a tropical island.

Kraus, Robert. *Herman the Helper.* New York: Simon & Schuster, 1974. Herman the octopus helps his sea creature friends in this delightfully illustrated story.

Lamorisse, Albert. *The Red Balloon.* New York: Doubleday, 1956. A lonely boy is befriended by a big red balloon on a string.

Leaf, Munro. *The Story of Ferdinand.* New York: Viking Press, 1938. This is the classic story of Ferdinand the bull, who prefers being peaceful to fighting.

Lionni, Leo. *Swimmy.* New York: Pantheon, 1963. Swimmy is a little fish who is left alone after his companions are eaten by a larger fish. When he finally meets fish of his own kind again, he urges them to cooperate so they can all live safely in the sea. The story is a pleasant lesson in the advantages of mutual cooperation.

___. *Tico and the Golden Wings.* New York: Pantheon, 1964. A warm story, with lovely illustrations, shows many ways in which each individual can be unique.

Lobel, Anita. *Potatoes, Potatoes.* New York: Harper and Row, 1967. A mother arranges a peace settlement between two brothers who fight on opposite sides in a war on their own potato patch.

Lobel, Arnold. *Frog and Toad Together.* New York: Harper and Row, 1972. Frog and Toad share a heartwarming relationship and many humorous adventures. Other titles, equally as charming, are *Days with Frog and Toad, Frog and Toad All Year,* and *Frog and Toad Are Friends.*

Lund, Doris. *You Ought to See Herbert's House.* New York: Watts, 1973. Herbert tells tall tales about his house when in reality it is like everyone else's.

Marceau, Marcel. *The Story of Bip.* New York: Harper and Row, 1976. Here are delightful images of love and freedom portrayed by the talented French mime, Marcel Marceau.

Marshall, James. *George and Martha.* Boston: Houghton Mifflin, 1972. The two hippopotamuses have a funny friendship and humorous adventures. Other titles include *George and Martha Encore,* and *George and Martha Rise and Shine.*

Massie, Diane Redfield. *Good Neighbors.* Middletown, Conn.: American Education Publishing, 1972. Mouse and Ratty learn to overcome their differences when disaster strikes.

McNulty, Faith. *The Elephant Who Couldn't Forget.* New York: Harper and Row, 1980. Congo could not forget that his brother had treated him unkindly. His wise grandmother helps him learn what is important to remember and what isn't.

Miles, Betty. *Around and Around Love.* New York: Alfred Knopf, 1975. Photographs portray the world of love. Many different ages and races are pictured.

Miles, Miska. *Annie and the Old One.* Boston: Little, Brown, and Co., 1971. Annie, a Navajo girl, has a special relationship with her grandmother and has a hard time accepting her death.

Minarek, Else Holmelund. *Little Bear's Friend.* New York: Harper and Row, 1960. This delightful book from the Little Bear series illustrated by Maurice Sendak relates how Little Bear and a young girl Emily develop a friendship and share tearful good-byes.

Nelsen, Donald. *Sam and Emma.* New York: Parents Magazine Press, 1971. A self-centered cat Emma and an outgoing dog Sam meet a variety of animals and learn some lessons.

Numeroff, Laura Joffe. *Amy for Short.* New York: Macmillan, 1976. Amy grows an inch taller than her best friend Mark and almost loses his friendship.

Oppenheim, Joanne. *On the Other Side of the River.* New York: Watts, 1972. Quarreling inhabitants in a village learn to live together.

Park, W. B. *Jonathan's Friends.* New York: J. P. Putnam, 1977. Michael tries to shake his younger brother's belief in the existence of fairies, witches, and Santa Claus.

Piper, Watty. *The Little Engine That Could.* 1930. New York: Platt and Munk, 1964. The classic story of a little train who finally succeeds by believing in herself.

Politi, Leo. *Moy Moy.* New York: Charles Scribner, 1960. The story tells of Moy Moy's life in a Los Angeles Chinese neighborhood.

___. *Pedro, the Angel of Olivera Street.* New York: Charles Scribner, 1946. A small boy is chosen to play the part of an angel in a Mexican Christmas celebration.

Problem Solving Series. Titles include *I Want It, I Can't Wait, I'm Lost, I Want to Play,* and *My Name Is Not Dummy.* Seattle: Parenting Press, Inc. 1982-83. This series of books deals with familiar problems of young children in relating with others. Practical ideas for how to deal with the dilemmas are offered.

Quinsey, Mary Beth. *Why Does That Man Have Such a Big Nose?* Seattle: Parenting Press, 1986. Each page of this book provides a common sense explanation to embarrassing questions children ask.

Raizizun, May. *Your Own Little Elf.* Wheaton, Ill.: Theosophical Publishing House, 1969. In a series of poems for children in the primary grades, the little elf is the personalized, happy self found in each child.

Ringi, Kjell. *The Stranger.* New York: Random House, 1968. This is a picture book about the reactions of a village to a stranger so tall that his face can't be seen by the villagers. After the villagers attempt to communicate in increasingly aggressive ways, the giant finally befriends them.

Schulman, Janet. *The Great Big Dummy.* New York: Greenwillow, 1979. Out of old clothes and other objects, a girl creates a playmate.

Seuss, Dr. *The Butter Battle Book.* New York: Random House, 1984. The confrontation between the Yooks and the Gooks mirrors the escalation of the arms race. This is an amusing yet emotionally powerful book. Unlike real life, there is no resistance from the people on either side.

Sharmat, Marjorie W. *Gladys Told Me to Meet Her Here.* New York: Harper and Row, 1970. Irving is waiting for his friend Gladys, who is ten minutes late.

___. *I'm Not Oscar's Friend Anymore.* New York: Dutton, 1975. Oscar's best friend tells all the reasons why they aren't friends anymore. Friendly relations are happily resumed at the end.

___. *The 329th Friend.* New York: Scholastic, Inc. 1979. Emery the raccoon becomes friends with himself and 328 other forest animals.

Sherman, Ivan. *I Do Not Like It When My Friend Comes to Visit.* New York: Harcourt Brace Jovanovich, 1973. A little girl is unhappy when her friend comes to visit and gets the lion's share of the toys and attention.

Silverstein, Shel. *The Giving Tree.* New York: Harper and Row, 1964. A young boy grows to manhood and old age experiencing the love and generosity of a tree that gives to him without thought of return.

Simon, Norma. *All Kinds of Families.* Chicago: Albert Whitman, 1975. This book celebrates the happy times and sad moments in many kinds of families.

Spier, Peter. *People.* New York: Doubleday, 1980. Incredible pictures and simple text explore the differences and uniqueness of people all over the world.

Stevenson, James. *The Bear Who Had No Place to Go.* New York: Harper and Row, 1972. Fired from the circus, a performing bear goes in search of a new home.

___. *Fast Friends.* New York: Greenwillow Books, 1979. In two stories a snail and a turtle have fun and a mouse and a turtle learn about honesty.

___. *Wilfred the Rat.* New York: Greenwillow Books, 1977. A lonely rat is befriended by a chipmunk and a squirrel. When his fortunes change he must decide how important these friendships are.

Stren, Patti. *Hug Me.* New York: Harper and Row, 1977. Elliott the porcupine wants a friend he can hug. At first all of his friends just laugh at him, but in the end he finds a huggable friend.

___. *Sloan and Philamina or How to Make Friends with Your Lunch.* New York: E. P. Dutton, 1979. Traditional enemies, an ant and an anteater, become friends and even help their relatives to understand each other better.

Timm, Dr. Stephen A. *The Dream.* Fargo, N.D.: Touchstone, 1982. This story, one of the Dragon and the Mouse series, teaches about disappointment and forgiveness. Other titles include *The Dragon and the Mouse,* and *The Dragon and the Mouse Together Again.*

Uchida, Yoshiko. *The Birthday Visitor.* New York: Charles Scribner, 1975. At first, Emi, a Japanese-American girl, resents having a visitor from Japan on her birthday.

Udry, Janice May. *Let's Be Enemies.* New York: Harper and Row, 1961. James and John are such good friends they even have chicken pox together. They have a hard time when one boy decides to be the boss, but friendship and sharing win out.

___. *What Mary Jo Shared.* New York: Scholastic, 1966. Mary Jo is shy about bringing something to school for sharing time. In the end she brings something special, her father.

Venable, Alan. *The Checker Players.* Philadelphia: Lippincott, 1973. Although they have different ways of doing things, the carpenter and the tinker work out a way of cooperating.

Vincent, Gabrielle. *Ernest and Celestine.* New York: William Morrow, 1982. Ernest, a fatherly bear, and Celestine, a sweet mouse, help each other solve the problems of daily life. Other titles include *Ernest and Celestine's Picnic, Smile,* and *Bravo Ernest and Celestine.*

Weiss, Nicki. *Maude and Sally.* New York: Greenwillow, 1983. Two inseparable girls learn to include others in their friendship.

Williams, Margery. *The Velveteen Rabbit.* New York: Doubleday, 1958. The Velveteen Rabbit, after most of his hair is loved off by his owner, is changed into a real rabbit by the nursery fairy.

Winthrop, Elizabeth. *That's Mine.* New York: Holiday, 1977. Two children who quarrel over a block learn the necessity of sharing.

Wittman, Sally. *A Special Trade*. New York: Harper and Row, 1978. Nelly, now grown, takes Old Bartholomew out for a walk as he once took her.

Wondriska, William. *The Tomato Patch*. New York: Holt, 1964. The secret of growing tomatoes helps two princes convert their warring countries to agricultural societies.

Yashima, Taro. *Crow Boy*. New York: Puffin Books, 1987. A strange, shy boy is isolated by his differences in a Japanese village school.

Yolen, Jane. *Rainbow Rider*. New York: Thomas Y. Crowell, 1974. The story, in which Rainbow Rider searches for a friend, has the qualities of American Indian myth.

Zion, Gene. *The Sugar Mouse Cake*. New York: Charles Scribners and Sons, 1964. This is an exciting adventure with a special mouse.

Zolotow, Charlotte Shapiro. *Janey*. New York: Harper and Row, 1973. A little girl misses her best friend who has moved away and reminisces about the things they used to do together.

NOTES

ADDITIONAL RESOURCES FROM ZEPHYR PRESS TO ENRICH YOUR PROGRAMS—

ME!? A Curriculum for Teaching Self-Esteem Through an Interest Center

by Jo Ellen Hartline (revised 1990)
Bring out the best in your students by helping them develop a sense of self-worth. *ME!?* has everything you need to set up a Self-Esteem Learning Center in your classroom. Ideas are adaptable to all grade levels. Grades K-8.
ZB04-W $16.95

A MOVING EXPERIENCE: Dance for Lovers of Children and the Child Within

by Teresa Benzwie, Ed.D. (1988)
Let this book dance its way into your heart! More than 100 exercises teach communication skills and self-knowledge, explore the world around and inside, develop creativity. Children feel good about themselves, establish values, and respect and support one another as they explore creative movement. Grades PreK-6.
ZB03-W $21.95

CHRYSALIS: Nurturing Creative and Independent Thought in Children

by Micki McKisson (1983)
Unfold creativity with this curriculum guide-offering more than 90 educational experiences-which presents the sequential steps to thinking and learning. Each exercise helps to develop creativity, self-reliance, and a sense of independence in your students' approach to learning. Grades 4-12.
ZB01-W $21.95

BEYOND WORDS: The Art and Practice of Visual Thinking

by Kathy Mason (1989)
You can link the processes of the right and left brain through visual imagery. Here's a "whole-brain" approach to improving your students' visual imagery in the classroom. This series of art exercises is based on McCarthy's *4Mat System* and is designed to reach students with varying learning styles. Grades 4-8.
KM01-W $19.95

PICTURE THIS: Teaching Reading Through Visualization

by Laura Rose (1988)
You can use visualization as a component to a literature-based reading program. This method of teaching reading links the brain hemispheres. Children who are taught with this technique not only read better . . . their writing improves, too! Grades 4-8.
ZB11-W $17.95

OUR ONLY EARTH SERIES: A Curriculum for Global Problem Solving

by McKisson and MacRae Campbell (1990)
Now you can involve your students in solving global problems. Here's how you can empower them with the skills and information they need to deal effectively with world issues. Each of the six books targets a specific world problem. Each offers eight lessons that teach not only important content information, but also diverse learning skills. Grades 4-12.

The Future of Our Tropical Rainforests
ZE02-W . . . $16.95
Our Troubled Skies ZE03-W . . . $16.95
Our Divided World: Poverty, Hunger & Overpopulation ZE04-W . . . $16.95
War: The Global Battlefield
ZE05-W . . . $16.95
Endangered Species: Their Struggle to Survive ZE06-W . . . $16.95
The Ocean Crisis (with Bruce Campbell)
ZE07-W . . . $16.95

To order, write or call—

ZEPHYR PRESS
P.O. Box 13448-W
Tucson, Arizona 85732-3448
(602) 322-5090

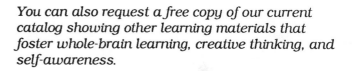

You can also request a free copy of our current catalog showing other learning materials that foster whole-brain learning, creative thinking, and self-awareness.